To Judith

Xmas 1968
with much love
Beryl.

The Gardener's Round

The Gardener's Round

Selected Articles from
The Times

Roy Hay

with decorations by
MARTIN BRONKHORST

MACMILLAN
IN ASSOCIATION WITH
THE TIMES

Published by
MACMILLAN AND CO LTD
Little Essex Street London WC2
and also at Bombay Calcutta and Madras
Macmillan South Africa (Publishers) Pty Ltd Johannesburg
The Macmillan Company of Australia Pty Ltd Melbourne
The Macmillan Company of Canada Ltd Toronto

Printed in Great Britain by
ROBERT MACLEHOSE AND CO LTD
The University Press, Glasgow

Contents

MAY

JUNE

JULY

AUGUST

SEPTEMBER

OCTOBER

NOVEMBER

DECEMBER

Introduction

LORD CAMDEN pointed out that it matters not what a writer knows provided he has knowing and communicative friends. Nowhere is this more true than in the world of horticulture. There is no more humble man than an old gardener, because he admits that, great though his wisdom may be, he is only beginning to understand how little he knows.

The complexities of plant behaviour; the mysteries of relative hardiness in plants; the changing feeding habits of the birds; the constant battle against pests and disease; the soul-searching problem whether or not to use chemicals; these and many more are the subjects that a gardening journalist has to ponder. Less worrying are the reports he has to make upon the latest aids to gardening for the old and the handicapped, and the modern techniques that can be used to reduce or eliminate the need for paid help in the garden.

There is so much accumulated knowledge that no gardener can ever hope to know it all. Yet as if this were not enough, so fast is the progress of technology that almost before the ink is dry upon an article parts of it may be outdated. The basic principles of good husbandry, however, do not change and the rhythm of the seasons follows roughly the same pattern year by year.

In the pages that follow are selections from the contributions I have made in recent years to *The Times*. They are not intended to make a comprehensive work of reference although I hope that when, for example, the family is discussing the idea of building a swimming pool, buying a greenhouse or remaking the herbaceous border, the suggestions I have made will be helpful. Inevitably there has been some repetition, for which I ask indulgence.

At the end of each month's chapter are 'Jobs for the Month'. All of us, even the most meticulous of gardeners, forget – we forget to sow the French beans or the sweet corn, or to order the bulbs for Christmas flowering. It is my hope that if this book is kept handy and thumbed through once a month the reader will be reminded of the jobs to be done and gain a few tips about how they should be done.

To return to my first paragraph; one of the pleasures of writing for a great national newspaper is that almost every week a reader writes to offer a suggestion – some discovery, an idea, maybe, for easing the work, some new way of fooling the birds or pests. This interchange of ideas is the very stuff of gardening and I hope that any reader who can take the time to do so will write to me – to criticise, condemn if you will, and add to our knowledge of this maddening, complicated but so fascinating pursuit we call gardening.

ROY HAY

January

Of all the months of the calendar January is the one that I view with the greatest apprehension. If there is to be a severe long-drawn-out spell of frost and snow it usually, though not always, begins in January. Apart from the inconvenience of snow, we prefer it to weeks of searing, drying north or east winds which do more damage than the snow or even straightforward frost.

But in the garden as with holidays much of the pleasure is in anticipation, and browsing through the catalogues, planning the changes to be made, the improvements, new plantings, and so on, is a pleasant occupation. There is time enough to sow the seed of an idea in the mind of one's spouse, and let it germinate.

The outwitting of the birds now becomes more urgent, and the tactics more subtle. The decision has to be taken whether or not to feed the birds. Some hold the view that if you feed them they will kindly refrain from stripping the buds from your fruit trees; others that feeding the birds only attracts more of them to the garden. Either way, we at home are soft-hearted in this and put out food and water for them.

Although the spring is a long way away, the days are lengthening if only imperceptibly, and the first snowdrops and maybe a winter aconite repeat the ageless promise that spring must surely come.

A few facts and figures

THOUGH I possess an extensive library of gardening books, every day I receive some obscure query the answer to which is difficult to find, although I know it is probably in the house somewhere. Some years ago I wrote that it was better to transplant evergreens in the spring than in the autumn – always provided, of course, that one is prepared to water them in dry spells until they are re-established. This was something I learnt at my father's knee, and all my life I have tried to do any transplanting of evergreens in late March or early April.

A reader wrote to ask by what authority I gave this advice. I searched through book after book, but nowhere in the 'classics' on shrubs could I find an authoritative statement on the subject. I just had to tell the reader that I had always found spring transplanting best, and hoped that he was content.

The kind of information that is most difficult to find is the quantitative kind, so it may be of use to record a few facts that are required perhaps only once or twice in a lifetime, but are not always easily available.

Take materials for paths, terraces, and the like. A ton of paving stone will cover about 9–10 sq. yds. Of course very thin stone will cover more, but stone an inch or so thick would cover about this area. A path or terrace paved with bricks laid flat will need about 33 bricks to the square yard. Incidentally, if you wish to make a path or terrace of bricks, shop around for 'well-fired wire-cuts'. This is the technical term. They are very dark purplish-red, and extremely hard. I laid some twelve years ago, and not one has yet shown any sign of crumbling. Gravel one buys by the ton, and this quantity should cover a path about 2–3 in. thick over an area of about 12 sq. yds.

For utility paths in the vegetable garden, around the chicken run, sheds, and garage, I use screened coke breeze from the local gasworks. It treads down in time to make a really firm path, and one can always rake it over now and then to freshen it up and discourage moss and weeds. If they do take hold, a dose of weed-killer can be applied. Coke breeze is much lighter than gravel, and I would estimate that a ton would cover twice the area that gravel would.

Sometimes you can buy from your local authority York paving slabs when a pavement is being renovated. They are not cheap, and I find it is usually cheaper to look for 'broken' or crazy paving. But there are places in a formal setting where square York stone would look right. Reckon that a ton of York paving would cover about 100 sq. ft.

Steps in a garden can look good, they can be easy to walk up or down, or they can be awkward and ugly. They should be wide enough, like paths, to allow two people to walk up them side by side. There is a formula which can be applied when building steps. A step has two parts – the 'tread' or flat part and the 'riser', the upright part. To have a step, or steps, that look right and are easy to use, ensure that twice the height of the riser, plus the width of the tread equals 24 in. It is remarkable how this formula produces steps that are a delight to use.

In the old days the gardening fraternity referred to different flowerpot sizes by the cast number – 60's, 48's, 32's, and so on, indicating that in each cast in the factory that was the number of pots made at one cast. Nowadays, thankfully, plastic pots are not made in casts, and in catalogues flowerpots, whether of clay or plastic, are described by their diameter at the top. But it is still sometimes a problem to estimate how much potting compost to order to fill a given number of pots. The most popular sizes for the amateur are the 3 in. and 5 in. pots. A 3 in. pot will hold about 10 oz. of a soil compost, and a 5 in. pot just over 2 lb.

Often one reads in gardening books recipes for mixing up composts, lawn dressings, and the like, by adding so much of this or that to a bushel. To make a box that will contain a bushel of sand or soil you have to arrange that it contains 2,220 cu. in. –

22 in. × 10 in. × 10 in. would be near enough for all practical purposes in the garden.

Fluid ounces, tablespoonfuls, and so on are as difficult for the gardener as they are for his wife in the kitchen. Nowadays you can buy a plastic beaker that has all these and many more measurements marked on its side. It is very good value at about 3s, because it is graduated for all fertilisers, weedkillers, insecticides, liquids, and solids – even for lime and grass seed.

You may think that you will never be required to work out the number of gallons in a garden pool. But perhaps one day you will wish to install a swimming-pool in the garden, and would like to know how much it is going to cost to fill it with water at perhaps 3s or more a thousand gallons. If the pool is square or rectangular, it is easy. You just multiply the length, width, and depth of the pool, measured in feet, and then multiply the result by $6\frac{1}{7}$. This gives you the number of gallons the pool will contain. A circular pool is more tricky. You multiply the radius in feet by itself – i.e. you square the radius – multiply the figure you arrive at by $3\frac{1}{4}$, and multiply the result by $6\frac{1}{4}$.

Even if you never aspire to a swimming-pool, you may want to have some ornamental fish in a pool. To avoid over-stocking the pool with fish there is yet another formula. You estimate the number of gallons of water the pool will hold, and then allow 1 in. of body length of fish, excluding the tail, to each gallon of water. Naturally, as the fish grow, and if you do not have a large enough pool, you will have to give some away, or make another pool. An even easier way, but perhaps not so happy for the fish, is to allow 4 in. of body length to each square foot of surface area. Remember, too, that fish will breed and the colony will eventually need more water.

There are plenty of conversion tables for temperature – Centigrade to Fahrenheit or vice versa, litres to gallons, yards to metres, and so on. But we still await a comprehensive little manual written solely for gardeners. It should contain, for example, such information as mulching – the weight of sawdust or old mushroom manure needed to cover a given area at a given depth among shrubs, or roses, or over asparagus beds. I have found that one ton of peat or sawdust will cover 144 sq. yds about 2 in. deep. Mushroom manure usually weighs heavier and I find does not cover such a large area per ton. Also, being rather lumpy, it is not so easy to spread thinly. But as it is very nutritious stuff to apply to beds or borders I put it on fairly thickly – deep enough anyway to hide the soil, and I suppress the weeds and give my plants some nourishment.

Books and catalogues give many varied recommendations for sowing rates of grass seed – anything from 2 to 3 oz. to the square yard. I have even seen 4 oz. suggested. In fact provided you are using a really fine lawn seed mixture, with no rye-grass in it, $1\frac{1}{4}$ oz. to the square yard should be sufficient. The fine lawn grasses produce small seeds; rye-grass seeds are much larger. The seed must be protected from birds – black cotton criss-crossed over the site on 6 in. twigs should keep the birds away. Most lawn seed mixtures are now pre-treated with a bird repellent, though this does not always deter the birds from taking the seed. If you are sowing grass to provide a rough meadow or orchard, or a hard-wearing lawn for children to play on, the seed mixture should contain a modicum of rye-grass. Then you should step up the sowing rate to 2 or $2\frac{1}{2}$ oz. to the square yard.

Even in a garden of only medium size it would pay to buy a fertiliser spreader. These excellent tools can be adjusted to sow grass seed, or to spread fertilisers, lime, lawn sand or top dressings over lawns or even cultivated ground easily, quickly, and with surprising accuracy.

Plant form

I DO not write often about plant shape and form. Perhaps having read a good deal about so-called 'architectural' plants, much of which has, it has seemed to me, been rather effusive and sentimental,

I have hesitated to raise the subject for fear of doing the same thing. But undoubtedly a garden does benefit if it contains a few well chosen plants that impress by their shape and form. If they give attractive flowers as well, this is an added bonus.

Naturally, the larger the garden, the more striking are the effects that can be obtained – for example the pampas grasses such as *Cortaderia argentea pumila* rise to about 6 ft, and *C.* 'Sunningdale Silver', an even more majestic plant, will in happy surroundings reach 8 or 9 ft. It must be satisfying to set fire to the old foliage in April, which is an easy and safe way of getting rid of it – much easier than cutting it down. If only we could do this with our herbaceous borders. Many people plant pampas grass in the middle of quite small lawns, but I always prefer to keep the middle of a lawn, even a large one, uncluttered with plants. Gradually over the years we have cleared almost all the beds and shrubs from the lawns, and this has made the garden look much bigger.

If you have a really damp, boggy area there are great possibilities. The enormous leaves and flower spikes of the giant *Gunnera manicata*, and the infinitely graceful but stately royal fern *Osmunda regalis*, are a splendid sight. Unfortunately osmunda cannot abide chalky soils. The gunneras are almost indestructible; they are all that remain now in what was once a magnificent water garden at Albury.

The ornamental rhubarb *Rheum palmatum rubrum* is another handsome foliage plant and does not need a damp spot. Where there is room for a small group of the plume poppy, *Macleaya cordata*, it will always attract comment with its fig-shaped divided leaves, silvery beneath, and feathery plumes of yellow flowers. It can spread by means of underground roots, and that is why I recommend it for an isolated position rather than for the back of a bed or border of herbaceous plants. Indeed, all the plants I have mentioned deserve to be given the dignity of an isolated prominent position.

The 'bear's breeches', species and varieties of *Acanthus*, are always referred to as plants of architectural beauty, but this may be because the leaves were often worked in stone in the buildings of the ancient Greeks and Romans. Be this as it may, a few plants in a prominent position are certainly very imposing. They need a well-drained spot, and in my own garden I have found them difficult to establish, having twice planted *A. mollis* and *A. spinosus* and lost them in the first winter after planting. Perhaps I should have covered them with bracken or straw in winter – yet in a garden a few hundred yards away they grow with abandon. The rose-red species, *A. perringii*, which grows to a mere 18 in. compared with the 3 ft to 4 ft of *A. mollis* and *A. spinosus*, is also a striking plant and my father grew it very happily in a border at the foot of a south-facing wall.

When it comes to choosing trees and shrubs, probably every landscape architect and every garden lover would have different ideas of what does or does not constitute good taste. If it pleases one to plant only British native trees in a country scene, so be it. But so many beautiful exotics have been planted for so many years that most of us have forgotten that they once came to us from across the seas. To some people the rounded shape of a well-grown hawthorn, or a horse chestnut such as *Aesculus briotti* with its deep rose flowers, *Catalpa bignonioides*, or the golden-leaved variety *aurea*, are more pleasing than the erect dignity of a lombardy poplar, or a metasequoia. Then some people do not like weeping trees, yet the weeping beech *Fagus sylvatica pendula*, the weeping form of birch *Betula pendula* 'Youngii', or the wych elm *Ulmus glabra pendula* can be very attractive in the right setting. So can the weeping flowering trees and shrubs – *Prunus subhirtella pendula*, or the deeper pink form 'Rubra'. The weeping *Buddleia alternifolia*, if restricted to a single stout but well-staked stem, is a glorious sight with its long ropes of mauve flowers.

When it comes to the choice of conifers, erect, columnar, or low and spreading, there is a wide choice. A visit to a good nursery or garden such as Wisley is really essential if one is to decide on varieties that will satisfy both partners in a garden.

Of the shrubs that are arresting by reason of their shape, none to my mind is more unusual or attractive than *Viburnum tomentosum* 'Lanarth variety', with tier upon tier of horizontal branches laden with large white flowers. But it must be planted in splendid isolation or its neighbours must be ruthlessly restricted to allow it to be seen in its full beauty.

Birds and buds

IN view of the ingrained British love of birds, I always venture upon this subject with diffidence. But I wish to make it quite clear that I and my family love the birds. We put out food and water for them in the winter, we have placed nesting boxes for them at strategic points, and our Siamese cat wears a bell on his collar to give the birds warning of his approach. So, you will say, we must take the consequences, and I am afraid, in my part of Surrey, the consequences are serious.

The bird population in my own garden and in the neighbourhood increases all the time. Nothing is now safe. The finches and sparrows strip the buds off our fruit trees, flowering cherries, wisterias, and forsythias; they nip off our crocuses and polyanthus, they take the black and red currants even before they have turned colour. They know exactly the moment to strip the green covering off the sweet corn and spoil the cobs. But they have not yet, thank goodness, shown any interest in our asparagus.

Mice, too, are a trouble in the garden. We sow peas and broad beans, also sweet peas under cloches. The mice think this is done for their special benefit, and burrow down to steal the seeds. We have foxed them by sowing the seeds and then covering them lightly with holly leaves, and filling in the trench. In this way we get a wonderful crop with no losses.

Guarding against bird damage is more difficult. All trees and bushes that may be damaged by birds we cover with Scaraweb – the rayon waste material that can be teased out and flung over a tree or bush so that it is covered with a kind of fine 'spider's web'. It is a wonderful bird deterrent, and I hasten to add it is only a deterrent – I have never seen a bird caught in this material, but they do not like it, and they keep away from any tree or bush that is festooned with it.

Of course with rain or snow the stuff becomes matted and needs teasing out again or replacing. One year we had a short spell of snow in March. I thought our fruit buds were safe, but the spider's web had become matted, and was no longer a deterrent, and the birds were taking it to line their nests. Every bird's nest I looked into in my garden was cosily lined with rayon threads.

It is always infuriating to find that the birds have stripped the buds of our flowering cherries, and I have tried to discover which varieties are less prone to damage. But reports from various parts of the country are conflicting. At Wisley, certain varieties of cherry seem to be immune from bird damage at one end of the garden, but are ruthlessly stripped at the other end. Furthermore, it is highly probable that because bird populations change, and the birds change their feeding habits – which they undoubtedly do – any selection of cherry varieties thought to be reasonably free from the attentions of the birds could well be out of date in a year or two, or would not be valid throughout the country.

In my own garden, where there are some twenty varieties of flowering cherries, the ordinary spring cherry, *Prunus subhirtella*, which twelve years ago was laden with blossom, has not had a flower on it for the past eight or nine years. It is too large a tree to protect with the rayon spider's web material which we use to protect pretty well everything now, and we have written it off.

The double white gean, *Prunus avium plena*, is never affected. Nobody seems to know just why the birds leave some cherries alone and take the buds of others. There are various theories. Some cherries make large rounded buds which are perhaps too large for the finches to deal with, although I doubt this. Others form their buds late in the season when presumably there are other and more interesting things to attract the birds' attention.

Then, too, it is probable that the buds of some varieties are more palatable than those of other varieties. I know one market garden where six one-acre blocks of black currants are grown in six different varieties. One March the birds stripped the buds of these black currants, but in a strict order of preference. They did not just start at one end and work through to the other, or tackle all the varieties at once. Obviously, some buds were more attractive to them than others.

However, the following is a selection of varieties which, while not guaranteed to be free from the attention of birds, certainly seem to be less attractive to them than many others. I would say that if this selection is not reasonably birdproof, then no other varieties would be in any particular garden.

The double white gean I have already mentioned. It should be the first on any list. Then the pale yellow, semi-double 'Ukon' is an excellent cherry, as is the large single snowy-white 'Shirotae' which produces branches more or less horizontally. These two, 'Ukon' and 'Shirotae', make an excellent contrast if planted together.

Still on the whites, there is the very large single-flowered 'Tai-haku', with coppery-red young leaves and truly enormous flowers. A very fragrant variety, 'Taki-noi', has white flowers, rather small perhaps but they contrast well with the reddish young leaves.

Then there is a really lovely double variety which is pink in bud but opens to pure white, 'Oku Miyako', sometimes known as 'Shimidsu Sakura' – also sometimes called *Prunus serrulata longipes*. It flowers late, and the flowers hang on long stalks. It was a parent of a superb variety 'Pink Perfection', and it is thought that the other parent was 'Kanzan', itself a very fine cherry.

It is sometimes objected that 'Kanzan' has been over-planted as a street tree in modern housing estates, and it is possibly true that one can get tired of seeing these trees laden with icing-sugar-pink double flowers, but I have never known the birds take the buds. It has an upright habit of growth, which means that it can be planted at the back of a border, and many delightful shrubs can be grown underneath it.

Another excellent semi-double pink cherry is 'Tao-yoma Sakura'. The tree usually known as 'Cheal's Weeping' cherry, *P. serrulata rosea*, is also a lovely cherry with double pink flowers, and it makes a very handsome arching tree, ideal for an isolated position at the end of a lawn, or in some commanding spot.

An excellent combination would be the double shell-pink variety 'Ichiyo' planted beside the double gean, *P. avium plena.*

Of all the cherries in my own garden, the variety 'Shosar' is probably the one we love best. It resembles *P. sargentii,* with single pink flowers which open quite early, even in March, and it has brilliant red foliage later in the year. One of its parents was *P. sargentii,* and it was raised by that great cherry expert Captain Collingwood Ingram. It flowers rather earlier than *P. sargentii,* and makes a rather better shape, although the round-headed shape of *P. sargentii* makes it highly desirable for any garden.

Hiding the hens

OVER the weekend, several neighbours started the old argument that it does not pay to keep hens. This my wife, who is responsible for the hens, hotly refuted, and produced figures to prove it. I keep out of the hen business, partly because hens are so stupid, and partly because their hen yard is no thing of beauty and I spend a lot of time trying to hide it.

Along one side we have a hedge of vertical cordon red currants and gooseberries. Along another side I am growing various climbers up a plastic-covered chain-link fence. But it occurs to me that if anyone is growing 'Queen Elizabeth' roses, it would be a simple matter to plant a hedge around the hens. Take prunings, pieces about 8 in. long, and bury them in the ground so that only the topmost inch shows above the soil. If the cuttings are inserted about 9 in. apart, allowing for losses, one should have a handsome hedge in two seasons. If they all grow – and over two years all my cuttings of 'Queen Elizabeth' rooted – one can always transplant some of them to another part of the garden or give them away.

Plants for an occasion

MAUREEN, Marchioness of Dufferin and Ava, was having a birthday party and she asked her guests not to bring birthday presents, but to bring half a guinea each to buy shrubs for a Sussex garden being created in memory of a friend. What a delightful idea. One day perhaps I shall hear what shrubs she and her equally enthusiastic gardening husband, Judge Maude, chose. Choice will depend on size, aspect, and soil conditions of the garden.

All this led me to ponder upon the kinds of plant one would choose to give to celebrate some family event, or to create a little garden of remembrance for a dear friend. Perhaps the simplest and most delightful would be a small heather garden, maybe with a simple seat, which would be colourful at all times if the soil is acid, but attractive nevertheless on alkaline soils if planted only with *Erica carnea* and its varieties. A few low-growing conifers, silvery or gold, and some autumn flowering crocuses or colchicums would add a touch of colour later in the year.

If one is choosing a tree or shrub to mark an anniversary – birthday, silver wedding, or the like – obviously it is better to choose one that deserves to be planted in a conspicuous position where it will be unlikely to become submerged in a thicket of other shrubs.

To take the large shrubs or small trees first. One of my favourites is *Catalpa bignonioides*, trained to a single stem as one so often sees them in Corsica. Better still is the golden form, but this has never been plentiful in the trade, and might take a lot of tracking down. These catalpas grow slowly, and make a lovely dome-shaped tree.

Then there are the magnolias. For a small garden, *Magnolia stellata*, which flowers early, would be ideal either as a specimen in a lawn, or in a conspicuous place near the house. *Magnolia soulangiana* and its white form, flowering a little later, and *M. grandiflora ferruginea* would be excellent. With *M. grandiflora* one tends to play safe in Britain and plant it against the south wall of a house. But I know specimens which grow happily free standing, because the house wall they were planted against has been demolished.

In the lovely little public park at Angers there are magnificent trees of this magnolia, with trunks nearly a foot thick, and in a bad winter it can be cold even in Angers. Like many other plants, *M. grandiflora* needs protection during the first few years after planting, so if the recipient is unlikely to give it this care, it might be wiser to choose something else.

Years ago, a friend gave us a plant of *Viburnum carlesii* to mark our first wedding anniversary. Unfortunately we left our previous garden in early summer and had to leave the viburnum behind. But over eight or nine years it never failed to reward us with a generous display of white, sweetly-scented flowers.

If the soil is acid, a rhododendron, particularly one that will make an imposing spectacle like *Rhododendron loderi* with its huge trusses of white flowers, would be a fine choice. Another splendid tree, and one which can be kept to any desired height by pollarding or pruning, is the evergreen *Eucalyptus niphophila* which simply shrugged off the frosts of 1963.

Then one would always be safe in giving a flowering cherry or plum. *Prunus blireiana* with its dark leaves and double pink flowers, which come before the foliage, makes a neat tree and is not too large. Of the flowering cherries there is a great choice, but one has to consider the bird hazard – no good giving a cherry that birds will strip if your friend lives near a wood with a high bird population. See p. 21.

Perhaps it is carrying the anniversary idea too far to suggest that the tree or shrub should flower about the date of the anniversary. But if one wishes to add this refinement, it is easily done, even in winter. *Hamamelis mollis*, or for my money its pale form 'Pallida', will flower from early December onwards, and after it one can choose a tree or shrub to give pleasure from its flower or foliage in any month.

Good resolutions

In the most well-ordered gardens, even where a meticulous diary is kept to remind one of the multifarious operations that must be done, each in its due season, jobs get forgotten. Sometimes we forget to sow the French beans or the sweet corn, but with a heated greenhouse one can always catch up by sowing the seeds in papiermâché or peat pots and planting them out after a couple of weeks. In fact, as we have spare frame space, we now sow our broad beans in this way and keep them in the frames until they are large enough to plant out.

Especially after a wet year we would be wise to apply generous dressings of a balanced fertiliser to all our plants – roses, herbaceous plants, and of course to any plots where we intend to grow vegetables.

One can, of course, approach this problem rather more cunningly and buy a soil testing outfit for 32s 6d. This will give thirty tests on soils from different parts of the garden and indicate what amounts of nitrogen, phosphates, potash and lime should be put on the soil.

Rain also encourages the spread of moss in lawns, even on light quick-draining soils such as mine. There is a widespread misconception that moss is caused by acid stagnant conditions. It often is, but not always, for there are many kinds of moss and some will flourish even on the lightest soils. So, too, with mares' tails. They are usually found in the low-lying parts of fields or gardens, but years ago in the station goods yard at Haslemere there used to be a huge 8 ft high bin, its sides made of railway sleepers, filled with sand, and at the top growing between the sleepers was a fine crop of mares' tails.

However, treatment with a selective lawn weedkiller in warm weather, say in June, usually puts paid to this weed. The moss on the lawn, however, should be dealt with now. A mercuric moss-killer I find gives a good control for about a year, for it not only kills the actual moss but the spores as well. There is no need to rake out the dead moss, it will disintegrate in time, but a good raking would probably be desirable for the well-being of the turf.

A rainy summer does not suit quite a few of our annual flowers, asters especially, and as an insurance we always plant a few short rows of tagetes and pompon chrysanthemums in the vegetable plot with the idea of transplanting them in bloom to fill gaps in the borders. This is a technique one could employ more often, especially for beds or borders that one sees all the time from the house, and which tend to become rather dull from late August.

These plants with their massive fibrous root system may be moved in bud or even in flower if they are well soaked the night before, and well watered in. If the border soil is dry it is best to 'puddle' them in – that is, prepare the holes and fill them with water, allowing this to drain away, and then put in the plants and cover the roots with moist soil.

The doctrine of expendability

NOTHING is for ever in a garden – all gardeners know this and are constantly creating new features, plotting and planning something different, but only too often they leave plants that have long since passed their zenith. All of us, I think, tend to soldier on with the garden as it is, with all kinds of plants, trees, shrubs and climbing roses, many of them old, misshapen, and really rather unproductive – just because they have always been there. So, too, we put up with features of the layout of the garden, perhaps a silly little bed in the middle of a lawn which has to be cut round by the mower, and edged up with the long-handled shears, when it would be much easier to grass it over, eliminate a lot of work, and probably make the lawn look more spacious and attractive.

At this time of the year when there is not much work that we can usefully do in the garden, it is worth while to sit down to some constructive thinking. I did just this a year ago, and in spite of my wife's protests, which I think she now realises were prompted mainly by sentiment, we removed a low lavender hedge, several shrubs that had obviously never been properly looked after and were bare at their bottoms, and quite a number of evergreens that were in the wrong positions. In their place we have put quite different shrubs that will give us flowers in their season, foliage for six months of the year or, in the case of evergreens, all the year round.

When we first came to our present home we made a rock garden, quite a large one. It looked extremely bare, so I acquired a dozen or more conifers, mostly varieties of *Chamaecyparis*, some of them upright columnar bushes, others pyramidal in habit, but all quick-growing. Some are green, some are golden, but all very attractive. These conifers grow fast. Most of them will make trees eventually 20 ft or 30 ft high, but when they get too big for their situation they can be removed and placed on the bonfire. Anyone could have ten years of pleasure from these conifers until they get too big for their lodgings. If the plant costs anything between 10s and 17s then the annual cost of the pleasure they give is not very much.

The principle of expendability in the garden need not be confined to shrubs. If, for example, you have a new and empty garden to fill, or if you want to make a shrub border, the obvious plan is to plant flowering trees, cherries, laburnums and lilacs, with flowering shrubs beneath, but these will be small and for several years will not make much of a show. So underneath the trees and shrubs plant quick-growing herbaceous plants or, if you can be bothered to do it, sow seeds of annual flowers. My own preference would be for such herbaceous plants as day lilies, varieties of *Hemerocallis*, dwarf michaelmas daisies, phloxes, bulbs, ericas, Japanese anemones, or even the hardy fuchsias. As the flowering shrubs grow and take over, these temporary plants can be removed, lifted and divided, planted elsewhere in the garden, or given away to friends.

We also have time now, when the weather precludes the all-absorbing work of garden maintenance, to look at the garden and think about the planting programme that we might carry out in the coming months. It is worth looking around to see if there are any walls or fences which could be clothed with climbing and flowering shrubs. We do not make enough of our walls and fences in this country. In some countries they use them for supporting pear trees, plums, peaches, apples and even figs, together with a great range of flowering plants. An empty wall to me is a challenge. Wisterias, forsythias, the winter jasmine, roses – all these and many other plants such as *Schizophragma hydrangeoides*, *Hydrangea petiolaris*, and in the warmer part of the country the bignonias – are well worth planting against a wall or fence. A small garden should have three dimensions, and the walls and fences offer us a third dimension.

Turning to trees or shrubs that have long since served their purpose, I am sure that many of us hesitate to throw them out because we have a feeling that it is not right to destroy something that has taken a long time to grow or simply because it has always been there. We have come to accept it as part of our own little local landscape. Or maybe it was planted by some ancestor, or was the gift of a kind and generous aunt and we have not the heart to get rid of it. There must be thousands of gardens cluttered up by scruffy old evergreens, leggy and misshapen shrubs, or semi-moribund trees. A good clear-out gives the opportunity to plant some of the more attractive varieties. An ageing tree might well finish its last ten or twenty years of life more profitably by acting as a support for a clematis, a honeysuckle or a vigorous climbing rose such as 'Mermaid', 'Chaplin's Pink', *Rosa wilsonii* or *Rosa moschata*. Ancient fruit trees, too tall to prune properly or spray, often produce little in the way of a worth-while crop and could be much more usefully employed as a support for some of these climbers.

Thoughts on the Mediterranean

IN the depths of winter it warms the heart to see in retrospect the flower-clad hillsides of the Mediterranean countries, the native flora so rich and varied, the cultivated garden flowers, great splashes of colour against the white dusty walls. The thousands of people who seek the Mediterranean sun tend at first simply to revel in the heat. Later they may begin to take an interest in the flora, and the next step is to try to identify the plants they see.

Here they have come up against an obstacle, because until recently there was no really authoritative and lavishly illustrated English book on the flora of this rich and fascinating region. But *Flowers of the Mediterranean*, by Oleg Polunin and Anthony Huxley (Chatto & Windus, 42s), with over 300 coloured illustrations, has amply filled this gap.

A trip to this region in early May is tremendously rewarding. On one such visit to Corsica, during a five-minute halt on the roadside, my wife found eleven different wild orchids in just about that number of yards of the verge. Glancing through the pages of the book, one comes across many old friends – the hardy cyclamen, *Cyclamen repandum*, and *C. neapolitanum*, for example. These, with *C. coum* and *C. graecum*, are all easy enough to establish in Britain, but it is better to buy growing plants than dry corms.

In these hot countries the ubiquitous goat has altered the course of botanical history, browsing insatiably, very often preventing the regeneration of large areas. Yet we can learn even from the goat because that beautiful but neglected shrub, *Spartium junceum*, pruned ruthlessly by the goats, is smothered with golden flowers in early spring. If you want early flowers, prune in autumn. If you want them in August and September, when there is no superfluity of flowering shrubs, prune in the spring. Would that we had more shrubs thus accommodating.

Foremost among the late summer flowering shrubs are the hypericums, which are not grown often enough. The varieties 'Hidcote' and 'Rowallane' are in the top flight, but I have found 'Hidcote' to be the hardier. Here again is a shrub that responds to much more severe pruning than one would normally give it. Leave it until the winter has done its worst, and then trim the shoots back hard. In this way a superb shapely bush will result, three or four feet high and as much through, and laden with flowers for many weeks.

The shrubby potentillas, too, help to prolong the shrub display into the late summer. Here again they are not so popular as they should be. We tend to think of them always as having golden or lemon yellow flowers – as in *Potentilla farreri, P.* 'Katherine Dykes', or the dwarf varieties such as *P. nana argentea* with silvery leaves, or *P. mandschurica* with creamy flowers and green foliage. But *P. fruticosa* 'Abbotswood', which makes a large shrub, has white flowers which it produces over a long period from June to September.

Jobs for January

THE prudent gardener will return to the habits of his forefathers, sit down and write out his order for seeds, seed potatoes, onion sets, shallots, gladioli, and all the odd bits and pieces of fertilisers, string, canes, stakes, and other garden sundries that he will inevitably need during the year.

Given reasonable weather, press on with cleaning up, cutting down herbaceous plants, working some organic fertiliser into borders, and clearing up fallen leaves. In the vegetable garden remove stumps of cabbages and other brassicas.

Pay particular attention to hedge bottoms, clearing out leaves, weeds, and other debris which provide shelter for slugs, snails and other pests. If necessary, water weeds with paraquat. It does not work so fast at this time of year, but it is still effective. More than one application may be necessary on deep-rooted weeds.

Finish pruning fruit trees and bushes, and spray with a tar oil winter wash.

Check everything in store – dahlia tubers, begonias, gladioli, onions, and the like. If the dahlia tubers are a bit shrivelled, put them in a bucket of tepid water for the night and dry them off well before putting them back in their store.

Give any beds or borders planted with spring flowers a freshen up – just loosen the surface of the soil. The plants like it, and it makes it more difficult for the slugs.

Check fruit trees, flowering cherries, wisterias, forsythias, and anything else that birds may attack. Either spray every fourteen days with Morkit, or protect the buds with Scaraweb. If you put this 'spider's web' on earlier, it is probably now a bit matted together, so it will need teasing out or some more should be put on. Once the birds start on a tree or bush, they can strip it of buds in a couple of hours.

Examine pergolas, rustic arches, fence posts, and other wooden items. A heavy fall of snow or a fierce gale may cause damage if there are weak spots, and give much needless work if a structure collapses.

Sponge the foliage of house plants with tepid water now and then to remove dust. To give large-leaved plants a good gloss, sponge on some Bio Leafshine after removing the dust.

Water pot azaleas regularly; they are grown in a very peaty mixture and if this dries out it is difficult to wet again.

Bowls of daffodils and hyacinths that have finished flowering should be planted out in some odd corner of the garden. Do not leave them to dry out in their pots or bowls.

Check greenhouses or frames to see that there is no broken or loose glass. Any gaps that have appeared through boards warping or shrinking should be stuffed with rags to prevent heat losses and reduce heating costs. Fixing plastic sheeting against the inside north and east walls of a greenhouse will also reduce fuel consumption.

February

H.G.R.

In a normal year, and it seems so long ago that as gardeners we had such a year that we have almost forgotten what it was like, February would be a wet month – February fill-dyke. Now the seasons seem topsy-turvy, but an open February, if it does not rain too much of the time, is a godsend. It gives us the chance to catch up with cultivations, finish the clearing up, and do those dull but necessary jobs of maintenance that have so often to be shelved once work begins in earnest in the months to come.

There is time enough to make new plantings, to lift and divide herbaceous plants, or do a lot of rearranging of plants that are in the wrong place; if February is kind these jobs may be put safely behind us leaving us freer to pursue the gardener's quickening round in March and April.

With the worst of the January bills paid up, one can again begin to think about some modest outlay on a greenhouse, a fruit cage or some of the other desirable accoutrements of a garden.

Weeding out the worthless

ONE of my father's favourite *obiter dicta* was 'Never look back, son. That way the lunatic asylum lies.' True, he was thinking of lost opportunities for investment and so on, but I am sure he, more than anyone, used to profit from his horticultural mistakes. I have seen him examine a full greenhouse and give a dissatisfied grunt. Next day, the whole lot would be thrown on the rubbish heap. 'Gardeners', he used to say, 'should be like doctors and bury their failures.'

Of course in those palmy pre-war days labour and money were plentiful. But even today we could all be a bit more ruthless with our failures or near-failures. There are thousands of plants that are not happy, crowded in, diseased, or just too old, and would be far better off on the heap. So every now and then my wife and I have a brutal clearing out. I mention my wife because I have found it wise to have her acquiescence in any act of destruction.

On a fine sunny February morning it is a good idea to take a stroll round the garden and decide upon eliminating any plants that are past their best or do not earn their keep. As a result several shrubs go on the bonfire and new ones are ordered. The first casualty on a recent inspection was a bush of an exceedingly spiny rose which for a couple of weeks only was reasonably attractive with its small double pink flowers. But over the years it became infested with ground elder and we decided to get rid of it. The only reason we kept it was because it was reputed to have started as a cutting from a rose on Rob Roy's grave.

We replaced it with a hydrangea because the position is in a north-facing border behind a wall where hydrangeas do very well. Our soil is just a trifle alkaline, so we do not waste time trying to grow blue hydrangeas. Friends often ask if they can apply a chemical to 'blue' their hydrangeas: they could, but it would be quite expensive, because it takes about 10 lb. of aluminium sulphate for each plant outdoors. In a pot or a tub 'blueing' is feasible, but not really in the open. The old 'Parsifal', a deep rosy-red, is still a good plant, but 'Hamburg' is a superb pink variety which, on soils which 'blue' hydrangeas, gives a really rich blue. For a rich deep-reddish colour, go for 'Ami Pasquier'.

A problem that has proved intractable with us and difficult, I know, in many gardens is the control of peach leaf curl. The leaves become swollen, red, and distorted. Theoretically this disease can be controlled by spraying in January with Bordeaux mixture or a lime-sulphur spray. This we did for several years before we discovered an old worn-out almond tree behind a laburnum. The almond was riddled with leaf curl disease. We destroyed it, of course, and recommenced spraying our peach trees in the hope that this time we would be successful.

But once again they were badly attacked, and the trees began to produce suckers, so we removed them. Once a peach tree starts suckering it is seldom worth persevering with it. There are too many other almond trees in the neighbourhood to make peach-growing a reasonable proposition – one can hardly ask neighbours to spray their almonds just for my benefit, indeed they are really too tall for an amateur's sprayer to reach, anyway. Strangely enough this disease does not seem to harm the almonds much, but then they are not subjected to all the pruning a peach tree on a wall receives, nor do they carry the heavy crops that one expects from a peach.

Another little job we do now is to mark with short sticks any places in the rock garden, or in borders, where we intend to plant more small bulbs next autumn. When bulb planting time comes there is no way of knowing for certain where existing bulbs are. With snowdrops, crocuses and winter aconites in grass it is even more difficult, and we have developed a technique for locating the present groups. We put canes in around the bulbs now, make a sketch of the area, and measure from fixed points on the plan to the canes. Thus in the autumn we can put the canes back again, and know exactly where to plant new bulbs. Winter aconites,

Eranthis hyemalis, grow exceedingly well on our light soil. Apparently they romp away in chalky soils, but my friend Will Ingwersen has tried unsuccessfully for twenty years to establish them on his acid clay at East Grinstead.

Incidentally, if you wish to lift and divide snowdrops, or move them to another part of the garden, the best time to do this is just as they finish flowering. One can buy living plants of the better and more expensive giant snowdrops, but the ordinary variety we usually buy as dry bulbs, and they do not by any means all grow. I planted 1,000 one autumn, but only about half of them appeared. Happily this does not apply to crocuses or winter aconites, although the miniature cyclamen establish themselves much better as pot-grown plants than as dry corms.

Happily too, the mice in my garden at least show no interest in any bulbs except crocuses. They dig down to find the bulbs even before there is any sign of growth, and at the first sign of trouble we put out traps, covered to prevent birds from being caught.

There are now so many birds in my part of Surrey that we grow all our soft fruit in one large fruit cage. Our raspberries and currants came to the end of their useful lives, so we made a new plantation with gooseberries and a row of Japanese wineberries in another part of the garden. Next autumn we shall remove the fruit cage from the existing plantation, and extend it to cover the new fruit plot.

This cage is quite a new and very ingenious affair. The uprights and cross-bars are of green plastic-covered 1 in. metal tube. The uprights have a cross-piece at the bottom to keep them vertical. The top cross-bars slot on to the uprights, and the joints at the top are covered with a neat smooth plastic protection. Thus the netting covers the framework without catching on the joints. The plastic Ulstron netting can be supplied in one piece of any size, but for a large cage I find it easier to have separate nets for the top and sides. These cages come in various sizes, all 6 ft high and from 9 ft square up to 36 ft × 18 ft. The largest size, complete with nets, hanging hooks, and ground pegs, costs about £30. They are available from most garden shops or direct from the manufacturers, Bridport-Gundry Ltd, Bridport, Dorset.

Given a little decent weather, sowing of sweet peas in the open or under cloches may begin, or if one has a cold frame they may be sown now in pots. We have been greatly impressed with the new Knee-hi sweet peas, which need little or nothing in the way of support. The flowers are large enough and the stems long enough to make very handsome arrangements, and a dwarf dividing 'hedge' of them is most attractive. In addition to the mixture there are now six separate colours named after Californian towns – Carmel, lavender; Los Angeles, crimson; Monterey, mid-blue; San Francisco, salmon; San Juan, white; and Santa Barbara, rose pink.

A trend away from dwarfness in seed novelties is marked by the new *Antirrhinum* 'Topper' mixture. This variety grows $2\frac{1}{2}$ ft high and flowers early. The colour mixture is good, and the flower spikes are excellent for cutting.

Joys of a greenhouse

AT this time of year a greenhouse is really most rewarding. In ours, we are pushing along bulbs for bringing into the house and we have an ample supply of *Primula malacoides, P. obconica*, cinerarias, cyclamen, foliage plants, and one or two handsome trained specimens of the sweet-scented white *Jasminum polyanthum*, so that we never have to buy cut flowers. Also we are sowing many seeds, rooting cuttings, and under the benches seakale, chicory, and rhubarb are adding to the variety of our meals.

I still hear people voicing their fears that a metal greenhouse is colder than a wooden one, and that there is a danger of condensed moisture dripping on the plants. There is very little difference in heat loss between wooden and metal houses, unless of course the wooden houses have wooden walls halfway up. But I would always choose a glass-to-the-ground house, if I only had the one, because one can grow a vast range of foliage plants under benches.

With the drip problem now eliminated in well-designed metal houses, and since the plants seem to have no preference, the question of wood or metal comes down to maintenance set against first cost. Houses built of real Western red cedar or other enduring woods should have a reasonably long life with little maintenance, but hot-drip galvanised houses need even less – aluminium none at all.

Considerations of materials apart, the width of the house is an important economic factor to consider. In every house one needs a path about 2 ft wide, so one must do a little arithmetic to work out the cost per square foot of covered growing area, whether in borders or on benches. Working to round figures and allowing for the path, a house of one popular make, 6 ft wide by 12 ft long would provide 48 sq. ft of growing area at a cost of about £1 a square foot. A house of the same length, 8 ft 6 in. wide, would give 78 sq. ft at about 16s 8d a square foot; and a house 10 ft wide by 12 ft long gives 96 sq. ft at a cost of about 15s a square foot.

In general, the larger the house the easier it is to manage – very small houses become exceedingly hot in summer and some of them are supplied with minimal ventilation. If it is possible to buy a house with ventilators low down in the sides as well as in the roof, the extra cost is really worthwhile.

Unfortunately many people enthused with the idea of running a greenhouse do not think the problem out thoroughly. They say that all they want is enough heating 'to keep out the frost'. They do not realise that to make the fullest use of a greenhouse, a few frames are necessary – indeed, I would strongly urge anyone who contemplates buying a greenhouse to consider installing some frames first, unless, of course, he can afford to do both simultaneously.

A range of frames – say a cold frame, one with electrical soil warming, and one with both soil and air warming – is a valuable asset. One can overwinter tender plants in the air-warmed frame, sow seeds of tender plants in it, and prick them out, then transfer them to the soil-warmed frame, then on to the cold frame and eventually to the garden. The frames can be used too for rooting many cuttings.

It has always seemed somewhat ridiculous to me to heat a greenhouse 7 ft or 8 ft high just to grow plants 1 ft high on a raised bench. We root our geranium cuttings in September, pot them up and overwinter them in our air-warmed frame. On frosty nights we cover the frame with mats or sacking, to conserve heat – which you cannot do to a greenhouse.

These frames may be used from a 13-amp socket, and stood right near the house all winter. Then, when the contents have been planted out in spring, they can be stored away in a shed or garage until required. A 6 ft × 4 ft frame, fully equipped with soil- and air-warming cables, costs approximately £35, and a 3 ft × 4 ft frame £29.

Of the 2,000,000 amateurs' greenhouses, how many, I wonder, are under-used? To get value for the heating, one should try to grow three layers of plants in a greenhouse – provided of course it has glass to the ground. All house plants, ivies, begonias, chlorophytums and others are quite happy under the benches. Then one can grow many kinds of plants on shelves above the benches, although watering can be difficult.

Even if the greenhouse does not have glass to the ground, the space beneath the benches can be put to good use for forcing rhubarb, seakale, or endive, and for storing dahlia and begonia tubers, and the like.

A word or two about temperatures. In gardening books it is still recommended to keep temperatures of 55° F. to 65° F. This is costly, no matter what type of fuel is used. By combining soil warming on benches or in greenhouse borders with air warming one can greatly reduce running costs. I have written about this many times, but I still come across many people who pay too much for their greenhouse heating. Often of course it is because the old gardener, who learnt his trade when fuel was cheap, just cannot believe that you can grow plants in an air temperature of 45° F. night minimum, with a root temperature provided by electrical soil-warming wires of 55°–60° F. Plants like this treatment; it is natural – the soil is always warmer than the air at night. So whether you are considering the purchase of a new greenhouse, or if you are looking anxiously at fuel costs, consult the local electricity board about installing soil warming.

Fences and bulbs

ONE advantage of the larger and more modern garden centres is the wider selection of screens, fences and so on. Hitherto, one could see different types of wooden screens and fences only at the premises of those firms that specialised in timber buildings, while other establishments had the latest ideas in concrete.

Choosing fences and screens needs considerable forethought. Usually they provide privacy, or shelter, or both. Let us consider shelter from the wind first. If the screen is intended merely to protect, say, a hedge or a planting of shrubs in depth for a few years until it takes over as a natural screen, and is not required to be a thing of great beauty, then wattle hurdles are probably the best buy and in rural surroundings are not unattractive.

Where privacy is important and something more sophisticated is required, we have to go to the more expensive types of fence such as the 'peep-proof' lapped larch panels or woven board panels. The former are the most expensive but the most durable. A dozen lapped large panels 6 ft high and of the same length would cost about £32, with hardwood or oak support posts extra. The woven panels of the same size are about £6 a dozen cheaper. These prices do not include transport costs if one is outside the delivery area of the supplier.

It is important, however, when erecting a screen, whether for shelter or privacy, to remember that a solid wall or fence acts as a stop to the wind and a tall fence offers a formidable area of resistance to high winds. So such a fence must be solidly buttressed against the winds with posts at an angle to the uprights – preferably, if possible, on both sides. It is fatally easy, as I have found to my cost, to underestimate the amount of support needed by a solid close-woven fence.

Then the wall or fence forces the wind up and over it, and the wind descends with full force on the other side somewhere about six to eight times the height of the fence away from it. In other words, with a 6 ft fence there will be an area of turbulence on the ground about 36 ft to 48 ft away from it on the lee side. This can be a very uncomfortable place for plants on a bitter windy night, or for, say, a bed of herbaceous plants in a summer gale. Where wind protection only is required, a hedge is a far better proposition as it filters and slows down the wind so that there is no area of turbulence. But of course one often has to put up protection to allow the hedge a fair chance of establishing itself.

When purchasing wooden fencing try to find a supplier who offers it already treated with preservative. This is especially important for the posts. And if the part of the post that will go in the ground has been pressure treated so much the better, as by this method the preservative has penetrated farther into the wood than if it is merely painted on. If one decides to apply a preservative at home, and it is possible to soak the bottom of the posts in the liquid for forty-eight hours, again, so much the better. Remember that creosote, an excellent preservative, can give off fumes from fences that may harm tender shoots of climbers. Far better to use a preservative such as Cuprinol which is not harmful to plants. But do use a preservative for all outdoor woodwork.

In town gardens or small formal areas in a modern setting the plastic square mesh fencing in various colours can be very attractive covered with plants. So too can the concrete open-screen walling units. In the right setting these 'honeycomb' walls can look very attractive with plants growing against them or in pleasing containers on top of the wall. There are various designs with triangular, square or semi-circular units, and these have been modelled on the Italian patterns and given Italian names – Milano, Pisa, Torino and so on. Very helpful leaflets about this type of open-screen walling may be obtained from The Cement and Concrete Association, 52 Grosvenor Gardens, S.W.1.

Now we should be thinking of the various bulbs, corms and tubers that may be planted in the coming weeks. First those for the owner of a greenhouse or conservatory in which the bulbs may be started into growth for planting out eventually, or for growing on under glass.

I am pleased to see that many of these plants are now being offered at reasonable prices – plants that hitherto were the stock-in-trade of only a few specialist firms. Of course, as with everything else, you get what you pay for and with these bulbs, the more expensive ones will probably produce more blooms. But I never mind waiting a bit; small bulbs will grow fatter with the years if we look after them. Take, for example, hippeastrums, or, as we used to call them, amaryllis. You can spend 8s 6d a bulb or up to 20s; there will of course be a varietal difference in size of flower as well as size of bulb. Lilies too are still available and here again there is an enormous range in price because there are so many new varieties on the market. But one catalogue offers the lovely orange 'Enchantment' at 11s 6d for three bulbs. It is equally good for the garden or for the greenhouse, or indeed for tubs in the open.

Then the arum lilies, both white and gold, are around now in fair quantity and they are excellent for a border, in a greenhouse, or for pot culture. Achimenes, too, are lovely greenhouse plants, and cannas at 3s each are excellent for pot work or for bedding out. All these, with care, can be increased over the years and are a good investment.

Among the outdoor bulbs there are the modern mixtures of ranunculus, the treated freesias which will flower in the open, 'St Brigid' or 'De Caen' anemones, ixias and of course gladioli which may be ordered now for planting in the next few weeks.

The 'scented gladiolus' *Acidanthera bicolor murielae*, white with a purple blotch, is a tricky one. It should not be planted until April when the ground has begun to warm up. Also when the corms are lifted for storing in the autumn they need to be kept really warm – we keep ours in a string bag in the kitchen.

One of the loveliest of all bulbous plants is the tigridia, available in a mixture of many colours. The flowers are all heavily spotted with red or crimson. They only last a day and are over at the end of the afternoon. I once knew a London commuter who grew tigridias in pots and when they were ready to open their flowers took them to his office to enjoy them during the day.

Growing for the pot

As Shakespeare had it – 'Sweet are the uses of adversity'. Here are some statistics. In 1966 we imported 105,000 cwt of carrots from the United States at a cost of £403,872. Altogether we imported 750,000 cwt of carrots costing £2,300,000. Of broccoli and cauliflower we bought 519,000 cwt at a cost of £1,500,000.

Why we do not grow more of these and other vegetables in Britain is none of my business, but it is obvious that devaluation caused all vegetables to be dearer – even the home-grown vegetables, because much of our seed is imported. True, Israel devalued her currency so the succulent fresh vegetables that she flies to England daily will not cost any more until freight charges go up.

So it may well be that many people will do as we are going to do, step up production of our fruits and vegetables. Also my wife, who looks after our hens, is buying another dozen. I firmly keep out of the hen business – I have little respect for a bird that is so stupid that it will not even go in out of the rain. But we greatly enjoy having the fresh eggs, although why three or four dozen hens suddenly decide to go slow just when we have a houseful of people at Christmas, and lay only a miserable three or four eggs a day, I do not understand.

Everybody must make his own priority list as regards vegetables. Also, if he needs detailed information about growing them, he should acquire *The Vegetable Garden Displayed*, price 10s 6d, postage 2s 6d, from The Royal Horticultural Society, Vincent Square, London, S.W.1. My own priorities are these. First asparagus, and if you are going to grow it, put down a really large bed. Of course, you can cut a few spears every day and stand them in water until you have gathered enough for a meal, but when we have asparagus, I like a lot of it. A. R. Paske & Co., Regal Lodge, Kentford, Newmarket, Suffolk, have bred a remarkably fine strain of asparagus, and they have produced a very informative leaflet about it. Although they offer two- and even three-year-old crowns, they strongly recommend planting one-year-old crowns, and I heartily agree. The younger plants establish themselves better, and get away more quickly. That, of course, applies to most plants, and we could save ourselves money, and get better results if we bought smaller nursery stock. This asparagus costs 1*s* a crown, bought by the hundred, at one year, but double that at three years. The best spacing for the plants appears to be 9 to 12 in. between the plants, and 3 ft beween the rows.

Next I put globe artichokes, and here again you want to plant about a dozen, so that you get enough heads at a time to give the whole family a feed. The variety we grow, 'Gros Vert de Laon', can be obtained from F. A. Secrett Ltd, Hurst Farm, Chapel Lane, Milford, near Godalming, Surrey, price 3*s* a rooted offset, post paid. They are sent out in April. Globe artichokes deteriorate after about three or four years, and they should then be lifted and divided.

Next, salads. Not being concerned with the housekeeping, I was horrified to hear that my wife is now paying 2*s* for a lettuce, and 1*s* 6*d* each for a chicon of chicory. Chicory is simplicity itself to grow, and mighty useful either as a salad or braised. Why we have to buy it from the Belgians beats me.

Sow a row of the Brussels, or Witloof, chicory about the middle of May. In November cut off the leaves, lift the roots, and pack them in a box of peat, and put them under the greenhouse bench, in the airing cupboard, or anywhere warm, and keep them dark by putting another box over the top. In about three weeks you have chicons. If you want green salading in midwinter, grow them in the light.

Now let us look at the lettuce problem. In theory it should be simple to have a lettuce or two every day in the year – if you like lettuces all that much. Before the war, Fred Streeter used to grow about thirty different lettuce varieties so that his employer, Lord

Leconfield, could have a different-coloured salad every day.

But with a little ingenuity, some glass coverage, and some electrical soil warming, one can have a few lettuces at any time of the year. Sow now in a greenhouse or frame a variety like 'May King', and plant it out under cloches in March. Then one should sow a very short row – 6 ft or so – in the garden from late March until early September, about every two weeks.

For the early sowings there are plenty of varieties, but I always prefer a crisp, crackly lettuce – the old 'Webb's Wonderful' is still a good one which hardly ever 'bolts', but I notice that George Roberts, Faversham, Kent, in his catalogue of vegetables for connoisseurs, is offering a variety 'Cornell 456' which he says is an improvement on 'Webb's Wonderful'.

Come August and early September, one should sow 'Arctic King' or 'Winter Density'. Then if you have a frame with soil-warming wires, you can have real fun. You sow a variety such as 'Cheshunt 5 B' or 'Cheshunt Early Giant' in October. You plant the seedlings about Christmas in the soil-warmed frame, and about mid-March they are ready for cutting.

Sweet corn comes high on our list. There are several early varieties, 'Sutton's First of All', 'Golden Bantam', 'John Innes Hybrid' – all are excellent but remember to plant them in a square block, not in a long row, as it is important to ensure that every seed on the cob is pollinated.

In the greenhouse we grow tomato 'Eurocross'; it is very short jointed, and we gather a heavy crop before we take the plants out, to make way for the late-rooted chrysanthemums.

The new dwarf tomato 'Primabel', raised by the French firm Clause, is being sold here by Sutton and Sons. This is a remarkable variety. It needs no stakes, it matures early outdoors, and the tomatoes are of medium size, smooth, and of a good flavour.

Peas, French, runner, and broad beans, leeks and celery are normal stock in trade. Last year we grew the 'American Green' celery, which is very tender and does not need blanching or earthing up. But severe frosts in December put paid to it, so we now grow a short row of the old type, earthed up in the traditional way, as well.

Living screens

IN a new garden, or one that is new to the owner but is either neglected or not very well planted, the obvious need is for plants that will grow quickly to provide an effect in a year or two.

There is the problem of providing shelter quickly in many exposed gardens, and in old gardens there are usually decrepit trees or shrubs of nondescript varieties which are no great objects of beauty. Even a new rock garden looks exceedingly bare for a few years and there is much to be said for planting a few conifers that will grow fairly quickly, in the knowledge that in perhaps six or eight years they will have to be grubbed up. Sometimes they can be successfully transplanted, but this is always a gamble.

However there are other shrubs like the dwarf lilac *Syringa pallibiniana* which will take seven years to make a bush $3\frac{1}{2}$ ft high and as much through. If it is then out of scale in the rock garden it can be moved with safety. My father used to say that one could move anything if one took enough trouble, and by and large this is true, but my doctrine of expendability holds that if you have had ten or fifteen years of pleasure from a plant that only cost, say, 1s or so a year you should not grumble. But along with the planting of temporary shrubs or trees one should look to the long term.

For example, if one plants a few fast-growing conifers for quick effect in the rock garden one should also plant an equal number of slow-growing dwarf conifers which will take over the function of giving height, contrast and winter interest when the fast growers are inevitably too big for their lodgings.

So, too, with screens of living material. It is easy enough to plant quick-growing hedges of prunus or cupressocyparis, but they will need regular pruning even after they have reached the desired height. If one uses a little imagination and plants in the lee of the hedge a selection of slower growing shrubs whose ultimate height will only be, say, six or eight feet and which will not need vigorous clipping, they will provide a much more natural screen. Also this screen in depth will be far more interesting at all seasons of the year than the solid wall of foliage provided by the hedge.

Eventually, perhaps, one will be able to dispense with the hedge altogether and with the labour of clipping it. Naturally it will be objected that such plantings in depth are only possible where there is room for a border some eight to ten feet wide in front of the hedge. In smaller gardens or in small parts of larger gardens the close-clipped hedge is usually the only answer to the problem of providing shelter and privacy. If only we had, as so many readers demand, a hedge plant that would grow rapidly to six or eight feet high and then stop.

But there are many plants that will provide effective and interesting screens and which need little attention. The varieties of *Buddleia davidii*, the viburnums, the camellias and rhododendrons on acid soils, pyracanthas; all these and many more can be used.

One of the saddest sights to my mind is to see the laurel used as a close-trimmed hedge plant. It has to be laboriously pruned with secateurs because if it is attacked with shears and leaves are severed the part that is left will turn brown and fall off. But, as free-standing shrubs the laurels can grow to 20 ft or more and are exceedingly handsome. The Portugal laurel *Prunus lusitanica* with its dark green pointed leaves and very bushy habit grows fast and makes a wonderful foil for a colourful flowering shrub as a neighbour.

Seeds for the greenhouse

WITH more than an estimated 2 million greenhouses in British gardens it is not surprising that the sales of seeds of tender plants increase every year. Nor is it to be wondered that the demand for such gorgeous flowers as strelitzias and clivias outstrips the supply. These are two fine greenhouse plants which can be brought into the home for a period when they are in full bloom, and it is to be hoped that the growers will step up their production. Both, incidentally, are easily raised from seeds, but take years to produce a flower.

A recent survey has shown that begonias, cinerarias, cyclamen, gloxinias, schizanthus, coloured-leaved coleus, primulas, and the busy lizzies, varieties of impatiens, are at the head of the list of plants grown from seed for greenhouses. About these there is little to say. The busy lizzies are probably the easiest to grow. The schizanthus prefer cool conditions at all times if they are to make neat shapely plants. If they are given too much warmth in low light conditions they will inevitably become lanky and 'drawn'. But then this advice applies in greater or less degree to all plants grown under glass.

Primulas, especially those delightful and dainty varieties of *P. malacoides*, need a dry atmosphere from October onwards. If the greenhouse is kept too humid, moisture will condense on the foliage and provide just the right conditions for botrytis and other disease spores to germinate and flourish.

All the primulas – the lovely modern varieties of *P. malacoides*, *P. sinensis*, *P. stellata*, *P. obconica* and *P. kewensis* – will grow happily and economically in a greenhouse with a minimum night temperature of 45° F. They may flower more quickly in a slightly higher temperature – so will gloxinias and cyclamen – but it costs twice as much to keep a greenhouse at 50° F night minimum as it does to keep it at 45° F, and almost twice as much again to keep it at 55° F.

So in the interests of economy it pays to have a good variety of greenhouse plants, either from seed or from cuttings, to give a succession of flowers, and to be patient. The only other observations I would proffer about the plants already mentioned are that coleus and possibly impatiens do not take kindly to B.H.C. sprays or smokes which, of course, are much used in greenhouses for the control of pests. Saintpaulias, too, I fear, are prone to dislike

B.H.C. I would not wish to be dogmatic about this, but since I have given up using B.H.C. I have had much more success with these plants.

I have also found that a small electric fan mounted high up in the greenhouse, pointed slightly downwards and kept running night and day, has had a remarkably prophylactic effect in keeping away diseases. The gentle air movement has dried the moisture off the leaves of my primulas, chrysanthemums, and other plants, and thus the disease spores have had no chance to germinate on the leaves and to penetrate the leaf tissue.

If one wishes to be a little more ambitious – without incidentally much more horticultural expertise – there are many more charming plants that can be raised from seed to decorate a greenhouse or conservatory, or to bring into the home to fill a *jardinière*, a copper jam pan or wine cooler, for a week or two. The blue *Browallia speciosa major* has large flowers in plenty in the winter months. The long creamy white spikes of *Celsia arcturus* are graceful and attractive. The modern forms of streptocarpus are also very decorative, and as they are perennial they can be kept going in the greenhouse for years.

Just for its graceful finely-cut foliage, *Grevillea robusta* is an excellent pot plant. Its large flat seeds seem to germinate much better if they are inserted vertically in the seed pan or pot than if they are sown flat.

Freesias, too, are very easily raised from seed. If the seeds are sown about 2 in. apart in deep boxes or large pots, the plants can remain in these containers until they flower. The seeds should be sown in spring, and the young plants in their containers should be placed outdoors until September and then brought into the greenhouse where they will flower in the early months of the year. One point to remember with freesias: they must be given the support of twiggy sticks. If the plants flop over and the stems are 'kinked', very probably they will not flower.

Time and motion

IT is surprising that in this age, when work and time and motion studies are part of the daily life of Britain, so little has been done in this regard in the garden. In commercial nurseries, and even in public parks, work-study techniques have been employed, but nobody seems to busy himself with the needs of the amateur. I have heard of a few efforts that have been made to solve such questions as whether a lawn occupies more man-hours than a rock garden or an equivalent area of herbaceous border, but I have never yet seen any firm conclusions.

Some years ago, the Tarpen hedge-trimmer company offered some calculations, which I have never seen questioned, which suggested that with an electric hedge trimmer a man can cut his hedges 5 times faster than with a pair of hand shears. The corollary, of course, is that one can go on cutting a hedge with one of these machines without undue fatigue far longer than one can go on wielding a pair of hand shears.

It has been suggested that if you have 200 square yards of hedge to cut – and this only means a hedge about 6 ft high and 50 yds long – it would be economic over a five-year period to invest in an electric hedge trimmer. You have to set the cost and depreciation of the machine against a gardener's time at anything between 5s and 7s an hour when trying to work out this kind of equation.

Of course all such calculations can only be approximate. There are variables – perhaps the garden owner enjoys the exercise and does not count the time, perhaps he has an old retainer who has to be employed anyway. But looked at as a business proposition with employed labour perhaps part-time, and paid almost at overtime rates, these problems repay study. Robert Andrews Ltd of Sunningdale and Hindhead, the suppliers of garden machinery, have recently made an interesting and detailed study of the cutting

performance of different kinds of mowing machine. They emphasise
that their conclusions are tentative and by no means comprehensive, but they do give one or two interesting indications that should
be borne in mind when buying a lawn mower.

Most people have only the sketchiest idea of the area of their
lawns. A lawn tennis court, for example, including the average
run back, would be about 110 ft × 55 ft, that is, 672 sq. yds.
Normally one would expect to be able to accommodate 7·2 tennis
courts to the acre. For the purpose of this investigation we will
do our sums in terms of tennis-court areas, or fractions thereof.
If the time and the distance walked behind either a push mower or
a motorised machine are of interest to the prospective buyer, he
should obviously ask some pertinent questions of the supplier
before deciding upon his purchase.

Here is an example. Using a 14 in. petrol motor machine it was
found that, walking at an average of 2 miles an hour, it was
necessary to make 45 cuts up and down a tennis court, and this
took 38 minutes. In the experiment the grass box was emptied,
whether it needed it or not, at the end of every run up and down
the lawn at a point about 10 yards away – either on a heap or into
a truck. The distance walked was 1 mile 138 yards.

It was found that with a 12 in. machine a quarter of an acre
could be cut in one hour, but just a third of an acre could be cut
with a 14 in. machine in the same time. With a 16 in. machine
just over half an acre, and with a 24 in. machine two-thirds of an
acre – these figures of course refer to petrol-driven machines.

When one turns to battery operated machines the time to
recharge the battery is important, because the amount of cutting
that can be done in any given day depends upon the mowing time
that a fully charged battery will give. For example, with a 12 in.
machine it was found that one could mow for about one hour on a
fully charged battery, giving a cutting performance of just over
800 sq. yds. But with a 14 in. machine one can cut for about one
and a quarter hours on full charge, and cover about 1400 sq. yds.
With the 18 in. machine the cutting time goes up to about one
and a half hours, and it is possible to cut about 2000 sq. yds.

It must be emphasised that all these times are very approximate; they vary with different types of machine and, where petrol-driven machines are concerned and the speed can be adjusted to suit the agility of the operator, the times will vary according to his inclination to walk slowly or fast. But this sort of information should, I feel, be available both from the manufacturers and from the vendors of equipment that it is claimed will reduce not only the physical labour in the garden but the time taken in maintenance.

When you come to think of it, a large amount of time in a garden is spent on moving things from one part of it to another. The best thing I ever did was fourteen years ago when I bought a large two-wheeled wooden hand truck with pneumatic tyres. It must have transported thousands of loads, and apart from an odd board that needed renewing, it is still sound – it even has the two original tyres. Maybe they still make tyres like that.

Then came the metal wheelbarrow, and ultimately the plastic type, and the plastic two-wheeled truck with the detachable body. You still see heavy oak wheelbarrows on sale today – who uses them? I cannot imagine, as they are heavy enough to push empty, let alone full.

Sometimes a friend asks me to look at his garden to suggest ways of reducing the amount of work. Quite often I find that much unnecessary work has to be done, because the rubbish heap, or compost heap, is at the farthest outpost of the garden. This did not matter, perhaps, when the garden was laid out in the days of cheap and plentiful labour, but it matters now. In many a garden it would be worth planting a few quick-growing shrubs like Portugal laurels to hide a dump for leaves or grass mowings at a much more accessible point. Too often the paths are wrongly sited for labour saving, and where there are different levels, nobody has thought of putting a gentle paved slope alongside steps so that trucks, barrows, or lawn mowers can be moved up and down with ease. Very often a concentrated drive for a few weeks on this sort of thing can save much time and temper.

It may well be that somewhere there is much more information available on time and motion study in the garden than has yet appeared in print, and I would be delighted to receive any documentation on this subject. Any organisation that has the time, staff, and funds to embark on a full-scale time and motion study on the garden would be doing a magnificent service if it would launch such an investigation.

Jobs for February

GIVEN a day or two with drying winds, and when the lawns are not waterlogged, this is a good time to give them a good raking. So long as I do not have to use it, a wire rake is a wonderful tool. But if, as so often happens, the master of the house has made himself responsible for the lawns (and probably little else) then unless he wants exercise, there are easier ways of scarifying a lawn. The Sisis equipment, rake, spiker, slitter, brush, and so on, may be used in a special two-wheeled chassis, and are not too hard to push. Or they may be fitted to various makes of cultivator.

Patching worn parts of the lawn may be done now by returfing. If a new lawn is to be laid this spring, either by sowing or turfing, press on with the preparations – levelling, digging, cleaning the ground, and if necessary providing proper drainage.

Protect polyanthus and primrose buds by stretching black cotton or Scaraweb over them. If not already done, protect buds of flowering cherries, wisterias, forsythias and any other trees or shrubs the birds take a fancy to in your garden.

Check on dahlias and other greenhouse tubers or corms in store. Cut away any mouldy parts and dust with flowers of sulphur, and throw away any that have rotted.

Pinch out the growing shoot of geraniums grown from last summer's cuttings.

Autumn-sown sweet peas in pots in frames may need stopping, i.e. pinching out the tip to promote side growths.

Start begonia tubers into growth by setting them in boxes of moist peat and spraying them with tepid water.

Sow broad beans in boxes in a frame or in a greenhouse for planting out later under cloches to provide an early crop. Alternatively, sow broad beans and early peas under cloches if the ground is fit to work. In any case, place cloches in position to help dry out the surface ready for sowing.

Buy some seed potatoes and set them out to sprout in a sunny frost-free place – a shelf in your greenhouse is ideal.

If the ground is workable, plant shallots and onion sets.

Keep a sharp watch for traces of slugs and mice, both under glass and in the open. Clean up meticulously all rubbish that may provide cover for slugs, and if their slimy trails are noticed, put down slug bait. Protect delphiniums particularly by putting a broad ring of sharp clinker ash around the plants.

Give fruit trees and bushes a dressing of fruit fertiliser, according to the makers' instructions.

March

For gardeners, as for hares, March can be a maddening month. It either comes in or goes out like a lion as a rule. It can be mild or miserably cold, unreasonably wet or dry. But the days are lengthening, there is time to do a little gardening in the evenings; and in most years it is an excellent planting month. One can of course still order plants for planting in April, but the later the planting the more care and attention to watering and mulching is necessary.

I always believe that whether one is making a new garden or remaking an old one, one should stop the constructional work in early April and concentrate on keeping the garden tidy. If one is trying to do too much in the way of construction or remodelling, the whole garden looks untidy all summer. Far better to call a halt and make the best of what has been achieved, starting the constructional work again, say, in August. So if one plans to build a rock garden or a pool, construct a pergola or do any work of this nature press on with it in March.

But do not be tempted by a few sunny days to think that spring has arrived. The ground is still cold. Even in favourable springs it pays to hasten slowly. Seeds sown a few weeks later in warm soil will germinate more quickly and the seedlings will catch up on the earlier sowings.

But now the daffodils and the forsythias proclaim that winter is behind us; set-backs we may have, but the gardening season is under way and we can only pray that it will be a mellow one.

Ideas for walls

MOST of us at some time or other yearn to grow a clematis, and there are clematis varieties such as *C. montana*, its variety *rubens*, *C. jackmanii*, *C.* 'Nelly Moser', and a few more, that can be quite happy against a wall provided their roots are kept cool, moist, and shaded. But a wall is not the site that a clematis would choose for itself. Ideally, a clematis would like to have its roots in cool shade and to ramble up through some tree or shrub where on reaching the top it can produce its flowers to its heart's content.

I would advise anyone who contemplates buying a clematis to discuss varieties with the supplier and obtain very clear instructions about pruning the different varieties. Furthermore, if the garden is on light, very quick-draining soil that tends to dry out during the summer, I would experiment, putting in a few plants to begin with, choosing exactly the right spot for them – somewhere where they can be looked after and will not be allowed to dry out – and only after a certain amount of success, plant more.

But there are plenty of plants to clothe walls which are not so difficult to please as the clematis. Unfortunately there are very few plants that are self-clinging and need no artificial support. Even with these self-clinging climbers the tendrils that cling to the wall are only produced on the new young growth, so it is necessary to lead the plants by some means of support during their first year, and hope that they will then attach themselves to the wall in their second year.

The varieties of *Ampelopsis* now known as *Vitis inconstans* or *V. quinquefolia* come readily to mind, as do the lovely bignonias, now known as *Campsis radicans* or its variety 'Mme Galen', the trumpet vine. Many a wall is ablaze with the vermilion or orange-red trumpets in August and September in the west and north of

France, and given a south or west aspect in the warmer parts of this country, they succeed here.

The many ivies, of course, are self-clinging and so is the climbing hydrangea, *H. petiolaris*, which has large, flat heads of white flowers, and gives pleasant lemon-yellow autumn foliage.

Provided we are prepared to put up wires on the walls or perhaps to affix the plastic-covered square meshed panels on battens, the choice of wall plants becomes much wider. Wistarias in white, blue, or pink are an obvious choice. So, too, the various honey-suckles, and here, if only one is grown, I would grow either *Lonicera henryi*, or *L japonica halliana*, which are evergreen. Of the two I think *L halliana* is the best, because it is very free flowering, sweetly scented, and if it is trimmed over fairly hard with a pair of shears every year it flowers magnificently.

On a very warm wall in a sheltered position, the passion flower, *Passiflora caerulea*, with white and blue flowers, can be very beautiful. It may be cut back to the bone in a hard winter, but it usually breaks again from the base, and if one has the patience it can be trained again to cover its allotted space.

Water is the key

I ONCE wrote about a simple way of subirrigating a herbaceous border and some wit wrote to tell me I had water on the brain. I replied that this was quite true as I garden on a very light soil overlying rock about two feet down, with a lane six feet below the level of the garden, running all along one side of it. We never have any surplus water in the soil and over the years we have evolved a routine for watering. If we have five dry days after the first of April we start watering and we go on until we have rain. We repeat the process all through the summer – five dry days and on with the irrigation.

I can, of course, sympathise with people who garden on clay, or in low-lying places where the ground is waterlogged for most of the winter. But even gardens in areas such as these dry out at times in summer – indeed a clay garden can become terrifyingly dry as the soil cracks and lets the moisture out very rapidly.

So I was delighted to receive a copy of Alan Bloom's latest book *Moisture Gardening* (Faber, 36s). In his first chapter he describes in great detail what water means to a garden. L. P. Smith, an eminent agricultural meteorologist, once said in a broadcast that all one needs to grow plants is soil, sunshine and water. Normally we have the soil, good, bad or indifferent, but it can usually be improved; we have, by and large, enough sunshine, but we never have enough water except in areas over 600 ft altitude in the west of the country, and in exceptional periods of rainfall. Alan Bloom has, of course, realised long ago that even the ordinary run of herbaceous plants need adequate water, but that there are many plants that need rather more water to flourish than they are likely to get in many gardens.

He has been experimenting for some years with various systems of subirrigation. Briefly he suggests laying 3 in. tile drains in a trench 14 in. below the surface of a bed or border, loosely butted together so that when water is poured through them it escapes at the joints and moistens the soil. In quick-draining soils most of the water will run away to lower levels and the plant roots will receive none, or very little of it. So he recommends laying a sheet of heavy gauge polythene at the bottom of the trench and laying the pipes on this. An alternative to land drains is punctured semi-rigid plastic pipe, one inch or $\frac{3}{4}$ in. diameter. This may be laid about 12 in. below the surface and in stiff soils would moisten a strip about 2 ft on either side of it – on quick-draining soils rather less. So one would lay pipes about 3 to 4 ft apart on heavy land but 20 to 30 in. apart on light soils.

I have not buried pipes thus deeply in my own garden but I have with great success buried a length of punctured plastic pipe in a wide circle just an inch or so under the soil. With this I can flood quite a large area in about five minutes and all the bog-loving plants I have put in have been exceedingly happy.

I can see that there is a considerable advantage in having the pipes far enough down so that water does not percolate up to the surface because, if the surface is kept dry, weed seeds will not germinate. I may yet bury it an inch or two deeper. This sub-irrigation technique is labour saving and also economical of water which does not evaporate as rapidly as it would if applied overhead.

The main part of Mr Bloom's book consists of descriptions of moisture-loving plants, giving their requirements of shade, soil and the amount of room they will require. The grouping of the plants in these nine chapters and the tabular information present the plants in an unusual and helpful manner.

I can imagine that the foregoing remarks will have been received with some wry amusement by people who have to garden on heavy soils that are low-lying or badly drained. Further, when we come to consider the vexed question of hardiness in plants, good drainage in winter is a potent factor. Very often a plant that will survive severe frosts in a light quick-draining soil will be killed if its roots are lying too wet. Conversely there is the scarlet *Lobelia fulgens* which will be killed on dry land but if planted in a bog will survive. It is these plant idiosyncrasies which, while they can be baffling and at times most irritating, at least make gardening an interesting challenge. It would be a dull business if it were ever reduced to an exact science, although one often wishes that some of the imponderables could be eliminated.

But the serious gardener, or even one who is just determined to succeed with certain plants, can do a great deal to improve the climate in his own garden – the micro-climate, as the pundits call it. Leaving on one side the problems of the soil and its suitability or otherwise for the particular plants we wish to grow, the three main considerations are shelter, drainage and the provision of water at crucial times.

It is not always sufficiently appreciated that wind funnelling through part of a garden can greatly discourage the growth of recently planted trees or shrubs. Some temporary shelter – wattle hurdles, wire netting and so on – often works wonders in getting them to establish themselves and grow away lustily.

Drainage can be a more difficult problem. Normally borders at the foot of an east-, south- or west-facing wall are seldom water-logged. They do not receive nearly as much rain as a bed would in the open garden. They are warmer as a rule and water tends to evaporate more quickly than from beds in the open. Also the wall may act as a sponge drawing the moisture up and evaporating it off. Indeed the trouble with wall borders is that they may need more frequent watering in summer than borders in the open.

However, in gardens that are wet and where pinks, pyrethrums, perennial scabious, thalictrums and other plants tend to die off in the winter, it is usually possible to grow them well on raised beds. If good friable soil enriched by some peat and sharp sand is put over the normal garden soil to a depth of a foot or so most of these plants that object to wet at their roots or around their crown will survive.

New ways with hardy flowers

MANY people predicted that with smaller gardens and little or no help, herbaceous plants would decrease greatly in popularity. But then we thought that greenhouse plants would go the same way, yet in both cases the opposite has happened. There has merely been a change of scale and choice of varieties. In greenhouses, fuel costs have forced gardeners to concentrate upon the plants that will perform satisfactorily at temperatures between 45° and 55° F., of which there are enough to satisfy anybody.

The garden owner who has to do his own work is acutely conscious of the staking problem, and dwarfer herbaceous plants or those that need little or no support except in windy gardens are the most in demand. One might, as a corollary, say that a windy garden is no place for herbaceous beds until a screen of shrubs has had time to provide shelter. But by placing beds in the open, away from the 'drawing' influence of a wall or fence, many plants will

stand up by themselves. It is true that in the pursuit of finer
flowers, as in irises and delphiniums, the raisers have produced
varieties needing cane support. But there is a good selection of
varieties that need minimal or no support.

The emphasis is now more on free-standing borders or beds,
not, as of old, necessarily in a long rectangle, and certainly much
less often against a wall, fence or hedge, which the old gardeners
considered obligatory – 'to form a background', they used to say.
There are several advantages to the free-standing type of bed. One
can walk round and admire it from all sides. One can, if it is not
too wide, reach into it for hoeing and dead-heading almost without
having to tread among the plants. Also, if one has no rooted
objection to combining a few shrubs with the hardy flowers, it
is possible to create in one bed conditions to suit different types of
plant. For example, on the shady side of a shrub would be the
place to put a small group of hostas, the yellow foxglove *Digitalis
ambigua*, meconopsis, or *Iris kaempferi*. Ideally most herbaceous plants
are best sited in full sun, but many plants will grow in shade
provided it is not too dense and there they can be kept reasonably
moist. With modern sprinklers this is no great problem. Besides
those just mentioned, there are the dead nettles, *Lamium garganicum*
with pink flowers, the yellow *L. galeobdolon*, and the forms of
L. maculatum especially the golden leaved form *aureum*; the purple
Ajuga pyramidalis, various geraniums such as *G. sylvaticum* and
G. macrorrhizum, *Aconitum fischeri*, *Helleborus orientalis*, and many
more that would be happy in a shady border.

Many people have indulged their personal idosyncrasies for
various colours – we have seen pink borders, blue borders, and so
on, but while some of these tricks may have come off I can honestly
say I never saw one that impressed me except the silver and white
border at Sissinghurst. This is a real joy. Here again one must not
expect the border to be a show piece all summer. There are times
when it is at its most attractive, but with plenty of silvery foliage
it is always interesting. White dianthus, the non-flowering form of
Stachys lanata – 'Silver Carpet' – *Artemisia lactiflora*, *Campanula persicifolia alba*, *Aster* 'White Choristers'; these and many more are at call.

The choice of shrub that will blend well with herbaceous plants needs to be made with care. The graceful finely-cut foliage of *Acer palmatum dissectum* is a perfect foil although it is rather slow-growing. Faster is *Viburnum tomentosum* 'Lanarth Variety'. But *Skimmia japonica*, the shrubby potentillas, *Deutzia elegantissima*, *Escallonia* 'C. F. Ball', *Spiraea japonica* and *Philadelphus* 'Belle Etoile' are all shrubs that could be used, and which can be kept in bounds by judicious pruning.

I should point out that I have been mentioning plants for rather special purposes. Besides these, of course, we have the whole range of the old faithfuls that must form the backbone of herbaceous planting – the paeonies, red hot pokers, erigerons, oriental poppies, lupins, bergamots, heleniums, and the like. These plantings must be entirely influenced by personal preference combined with a careful consideration of site and performance at any particular time.

Obviously, the choice of plants for an herbaceous bed or border must be governed by the desired flowering period – the most difficult is the one intended to provide interest from April to October, the easiest are those expected to give a blaze of glory for a short period, say in June or July. When planning parties in the summer, the last week of June or the first week of July are probably the best to choose, as the temperature should be agreeable enough outside, and the risk of a washout is comparatively less. Inquiries and the meteorological records pointed unequivocally to the last Sunday in June as the best bet for our 'Gardeners' Sunday' for gardeners' charities. For eleven successive years it was on the whole fine, warm and dry. Only in 1967 was there rain over almost the whole country.

Now to consider the actual planning of a bed or border. Here one can lay down only a few guide lines. To achieve balance one should choose for the tallest plants those that will grow to a height of half the width of the border. Allow about five plants to each square yard. Plants which make a larger lateral spread need to be planted more thinly. It is tempting when planning a border to try to grade the plants up smoothly from the almost prostrate kinds in the front to the taller varieties at the back, or in the case of an island bed, to put the taller plants in the middle. But even if one manages to put the right plants in exactly the right place, the result is flat and not very interesting. Far better to vary the contours a little, bring the odd groups of taller plants a little nearer the front here and there, allow a drift of a dwarf plant such as *Sedum caeruleum* to run back among taller plants and so on.

As to the number of any particular variety to plant, I would suggest three or five, according to the length and width of the border. One must remember that when, say, oriental poppies finish flowering, they leave a nasty gap. True, they can be cut down after flowering and an obliging neighbour, such as a bergamot, a phlox or a red hot poker, will take over a certain amount of the poppies' room. Planning herbaceous plantings is a fascinating exercise. We shall never achieve perfection, but improving on last year, moving plants around, substituting new ones for those that fail to live up to expectations – this is the stuff of gardening.

Swimming-pools

HAVING two young daughters and their various friends, I have had the subject of installing a swimming-pool in the garden tossed around in family discussions for many years. Fortunately for me, neither daughter has been madly keen on swimming. We have as a family been lucky enough to spend our holidays in the past ten years in France or Corsica, and we all like our swimming conditions to be warm. Also we are blessed with friends in the neighbourhood who have very fine swimming-pools which we have been invited to use, and which, indeed, we have gladly used during oppressively hot periods. But I have found it very interesting to investigate the possibilities, the alternatives, and the costs of installing a pool. The Association of Swimming Pool Contractors Ltd, 61 Holywell Road, Watford, Herts., has wisely, and in common with other trade associations, prepared minimum standards for swimming-pools, and I would suggest that as a first step it would be worth sending 10s 6d for this book of technical information.

From my own experience of making concrete-walled garden pools I agree with the association in their contention that, like the installation of electrical circuits, this is no field of endeavour for the amateur handyman. As far as I can see a swimming-pool is going to be an expensive item, but if there are enough members of the family who will enjoy it, then it will be worth while.

Broadly, swimming-pools fall into two categories, those sunk into the ground, and those erected above ground level.

Of the former type, one can choose the prefabricated fibre glass pools, installed after excavation, and these vary in size from about 26 ft × 12 ft to 40 ft × 20 ft. But the orthodox reinforced concrete type of pool is still very popular, and the pool constructors have developed new techniques both for constructing the pools and for rendering the inside surfaces to provide an attractive finish. It is most important to go to a specialist firm. I know of one case where a local firm made a pool, but did not reinforce the concrete bottom. This caused a vast amount of trouble, because the pool leaked and had to have a new base.

The size of the pool must depend upon the price one is prepared to pay, but for keen swimmers one should think in terms of a pool, say, 40 ft × 20 ft and 6 ft 6 in. deep at one end. If the family contains keen divers it would be wise to deepen the deep end to 7 ft 6 in.

The 'above ground' pools are becoming popular because they require no major excavation. One type, 4 ft deep, 30 ft long of irregular shape, is 14 ft wide at its widest point and 10 ft at its narrowest. Delivered, erected and equipped with plumbing for filtration equipment, automatic surface skimmer, a sun deck and steps, the price is around £680.

When it comes to estimating costs of installing a traditional type of sunken concrete-walled pool, prices can vary enormously. But if serious specialist firms are employed the cost of basic work of making and lining the pool should not vary too much. The location and any peculiarities of the site, and the travelling time involved must of course be taken into consideration. One can also embark upon all kinds of refinements – electric heating of the pool, built-in purification equipment, prefabricated plastic buildings covering the pool and thus enabling it to be used in all weathers. The latest refinement is the sauna bath as an adjunct. Another worthwhile accessory is a large plastic or canvas cover which will catch leaves or other debris and is readily removable.

I am somewhat reluctant about suggesting prices for any garden commodity as, since devaluation, these tend to vary almost daily. Obviously, some firms charge more than others. If you have a specialist firm in the neighbourhood, they will probably be able to make you a pool more cheaply than if you employ a firm from a long way away. But in any case, the heating and purification equipment should cost about the same whoever installs the pool.

So to give you an approximate idea of what a well finished, reinforced concrete pool, made and fully equipped, would cost I have taken the prices from one of the best known specialist firms. They are as follows:

Pool constructed *in situ* 40 ft × 20 ft × 3 ft 6 in. to 6 ft 6 in. depth:

Shell, coping and rendering, £1500; heater, 26,880 gallons, £365; chlorinator, £50. Extras for vacuum cleaner, £30; underwater light, £30; diving-board, 12 ft, £40; one set of steps, £30; filter, £300; plus installation costs.

I am informed that the item 'installation costs' of the heating and other equipment is difficult to assess, but could be roughly £250. Allowing for my notorious inability to add up the simplest sums correctly, I make the total cost of a really first-class pool of this type to be around £2500.

Such a pool, or any efficient pool, gives enormous pleasure to a family where children and friends will use it. Attached to a family house it is obviously a good investment. When all the children have left the nest and father and mother decide to move to a more modest house, the prospective buyer will be a family man, and the swimming-pool may well be the factor which decides him to purchase the property.

For this reason if I were considering the acquisition of a swimming-pool, I would install a really permanent job, fully equipped with heating and filtration plants, with a neatly paved surround, well landscaped with shrubs and plants. I would also have an attractive summer house where the swimmers can change and the non-swimming parents of visiting children can sip their pre-lunch aperitifs in comfort. One very important point to watch is that paving surrounding the pool is laid on a very well consolidated base, otherwise after a year or two it may become uneven.

Planting for the winter

THE sun glinting on a massive bush of pussy willow covered with catkins reminded me about the 'berried treasure', as the late Frank Kingdon Ward so aptly called it. It is easy to imagine, when reading a book about the horticultural delights that one can have in the winter, that the garden can be just as much a blaze of colour as in the summer.

Of course, it is not so. But if we consciously plant a selection of shrubs, trees, and other plants for their effect in autumn and winter, the dividend can be very worth while. I am not at the moment thinking of the autumn and winter flowers – the viburnums, witch hazels, the forsythias, mahonias, the winter-flowering bulbs, and all the other plants that brave the worst of our weather and bring us so much pleasure. These are indispensable. But there is still plenty of time to plant a few flowering shrubs for winter and early spring. Perhaps it would be worth while to make it a rule to plant one or two every year. For weeks my wife and I have made a daily visit to admire a bush of the white form of *Daphne mezereum* laden with sweetly scented flowers, a gift years ago from that great gardener and gardening journalist, the late

A. T. Johnson. As long as his daphne lives we shall be reminded of him every winter.

We are glad too that we planted so many winter-flowering heathers, all the forms of *Erica carnea* we could find. Ours is a slightly alkaline soil, so we concentrated on these forms which grow on any soil.

If our garden had been acid, we would have enjoyed many other lovely plants now denied to us; we would have probably planted many heaths and heathers for summer and winter flowering, but we would not have had so much colour just when we need it most, in February and March.

Returning to the berries, the hips and haws, the ornamental fruits and catkins, the objection will be raised that just as the ornamental fruits are at their best, the birds move in and ruin the effect. But the harmless bird deterrent spray Morkit has proved highly successful in many instances in protecting ornamental berries for long periods. And perhaps before newly planted trees or shrubs are in full bearing, the compound may be further improved.

I think first of the genus *Cotoneaster*. Starting with the lowest, there is *C. horizontalis*, which will cover a large area either flat on the ground or up and over a low wall. It seldom fails to oblige with a rich crop of scarlet berries in autumn, and one of my own bushes is intergrown with the yellow *Jasminum nudiflorum* so we usually have the red berries and golden flowers together. There is also a variegated form of *C. horizontalis* which is very attractive. A semi-prostrate variety, *C. conspicua decora*, has pendulous branches, usually smothered with scarlet berries, and in many gardens the birds leave them alone. But where birds are concerned I am always fearful that they may change their feeding habits, or that a new variety of bird may arrive in the neighbourhood. Of the taller cotoneasters, *C.* 'Cornubia' will grow 12 ft high and about as much through, and carries masses of red berries.

Wherever possible I avoid plants with spines or thorns, and I have no berberis species or varieties in my garden. But it is perhaps poorer without *B. stenophylla*, a good hedge plant with yellow flowers and purple berries, and *B. thunbergii*, with reddish-yellow flowers and scarlet berries. If we had to deter local children from paying us unwanted visits, these two plants would make fearsome hedges in time.

The crab apples are always worth their space. *Malus* 'John Downie', with scarlet fruits, and *M.* 'Golden Hornet' is always handsome, festooned with its tapering golden fruits. The pyracanthas make handsome specimens – *P. watereri*, 10 ft high, or *P. atalantioides*, double that height, both with red berries, or *P. angustifolia*, with orange fruits.

For hips, the rose 'Allen Chandler', climber, obliges with scarlet, as does *Rosa rubiginosa*. The thorn *Crataegus carrierei* has lovely orange fruits, and – very unusual – *Callicarpa giraldiana* has violet berries.

Turning again to the catkins, we think first of the willows, species and varieties of *Salix*. The ordinary goat willow, *Salix caprea* with the yellow catkins, its weeping variety *pendula*, and *S. daphnoides* 'Aglaia' with silver catkins, are worth growing. Then we have the hazels, forms of *Corylus*. Here there are two all-purpose, all-soil forms – *Corylus maxima* 'Purpurea' with dark leaves and purple catkins, and the twisted stemmed *C. avellana* 'Contorta', with fawn coloured catkins. These are bound to attract attention.

There are many more plants, of course, that we can plant for out-of-season beauty. As the years go by they grow in beauty and interest, and are a wonderful investment.

Nurseries and Garden Centres

THE concept of the garden centre is excellent in many ways, but it has its limitations, and if, as seems inevitable, the traditional methods of marketing horticultural products must to some extent change, the changes may not always be for the better. First it is necessary to define the term 'garden centre'. There is a tendency for this term to be rather devalued when a shop or store sets up a display of tools, fertilisers, and so on, and proudly proclaims its 'garden centre', useful though its display may be.

A comprehensive garden centre must obviously offer a wide range of plants in addition to the range of machines and garden sundries. In certain overseas countries, where the weather is more predictable, garden centres are easier to run commercially and profitably. Here again they vary enormously in their scope. Just outside Paris, at Plaisir, the firm of Clause have laid out an enormous centre with a dozen specimen small gardens of widely different design.

Some obviously would not greatly impress the more sophisticated British gardener, but for each garden one can obtain a planting plan, showing how many of each type of plant have been used, and the cost of each plant; also the quantities of paving, gravel, or whatever else has been used in the garden. This centre, together with its huge modern display building, is the most ambitious I have seen in Europe, or even in the United States, but then I know there are far larger centres in New England than I have been able to visit.

Here, garden centres, some of them large and very well stocked, have appeared in many parts of the country. The largest of all at Syon Park near Brentford contains demonstration gardens of different kinds in addition to large-scale collections of almost all the different types of plant the amateur wishes to grow.

Now let us consider the advantages of buying at a garden centre. One can examine the plants either grown in containers or bedded in peat, and see exactly what one is buying. Prices are understandably slightly higher than at a normal nursery because the cost of the container and regular watering has to be added. On the other hand, there are no packing and transport charges, because you pick up your plants, pack them in the car, and take them home.

It is, of course, always desirable to prepare well the planting positions for trees, shrubs, roses and the like, whether they are coming from a nursery or from a garden centre. Peat, manure, bone meal, and so on should be worked into the site, preferably a few weeks in advance of planting.

But with container-grown plants which one can buy at almost any time during the year, the initial preparation is even more important. Planting, say from late April onwards, to be successful calls for even more moisture retaining peat or the like, mulching and watering, than would be necessary if planting is carried out from October to March.

There is a trend, probably irreversible now, to reduce the number of varieties of plants offered to the gardening public. Perhaps in these days of smaller gardens it is no longer necessary to have the choice of 50 apples, and 2 or 3 dozen pears. Certainly, apart from the larger specialist firms, pure economics of production will bring about a concentration upon the most popular varieties. It is a trend that one must regret, because our gardens must inevitably become less varied in their planting. So I venture to suggest that while it is sensible to patronise the garden centres, it is also still sensible to buy from the well-established nurseries who catalogue a wide range of plants.

It is often objected that plants are expensive, but in comparison with other commodities their prices have not risen commensurately. Even if prices do have to rise a little, they will still represent good value. The nurseryman's costs, labour, petrol, catalogue printing, postage, and so on, have all risen smartly since the war. Also, the established nurseries spend a lot of time in giving advice to customers both by letter and at flower shows up and down the country. They usually replace willingly any plants that have failed, at considerably reduced prices, or in some cases even at no cost. These are services that many thousands of customers value.

I mentioned apropos asparagus that one-year-old plants usually establish themselves better than older crowns, and that often the smaller and younger specimens of shrubs did the same. This is usually true. Quite often a young, vigorous shrub will in a year or two make as good a plant or better than an older and consequently more expensive specimen. But with plants, as with most things in life, you get what you pay for, and there is a world of difference between a well-grown young shrub with a good root system, and a shrub that has been poorly grown and rushed on to the market with only a meagre complement of roots.

It takes time to learn how to recognise quality in plants, but it is worth learning. Of course, no cow gives all cream all the time, and no nurseryman can produce all first-quality plants. But those who value their good name will, if top size plants are not available, offer a smaller specimen at a lower price still representing excellent value. There are now British Standards for nursery stock, and many firms market their plants under these, and often higher, standards.

It is not generally realised how long it takes to produce a good specimen of a grafted tree or shrub. First the stock has to be raised from seed, anything from two to four years; it has to be transplanted to the field and grown on for a year, budded or grafted, staked, tied and pruned as it grows – all this takes another four years. It will need hoeing or weeding, and fertilisers, and finally lifting. A tree thus produced costing, say 40s to the customer is four times as expensive as in pre-war days, but nursery wages have gone up six and a half times, and there have been many increases in the cost of materials and fuel, not to mention direct and indirect taxation.

Now we must consider the vexed question of transport, its cost, and the possibility of vexatious delays. Many nurseries now deliver over quite a large area by their own transport. But gardeners who live near each other could often help themselves by combining their orders in one consignment. Considerable savings result in this way. Also forethought, ordering the bulk of one's requirements at one time and not just sending off for a plant of this or that as the spirit moves us, much reduces packing and transport charges.

Seeking out the best

IT pays to do a bit of homework before buying plants. For instance, among shrubs there are many fine forms that are only gradually coming into large-scale production. As a superb ground cover, the periwinkle can subjugate almost any weed. There are about a dozen varieties, some with variegated leaves, some with double flowers, although the double white form seems to have become very scarce. One of my favourites is *Vinca minor superba* which is very free-flowering and makes an even denser carpet of foliage than 'Bowles' variety' which has been so popular for many years.

Then take sun roses, the varieties of helianthemum. If you go to the office every day choose the double varieties – the single forms will probably have shed their petals by the time you come home in the evening. Sun roses need an annual trimming after flowering because they tend to become a trifle leggy.

The lovely lilac *Ceanothus* 'Gloire de Versailles' which needs clipping back each spring is a good plant, but 'Topaz' is a superior colour and makes a neater plant. Pampas grasses vary a good deal in the size and fluffiness of their silvery plumes and *Cortaderia* 'Sunningdale Silver' is a notable improvement.

Once more we have to learn a new name for an old favourite, for the shrubby veronicas are now known as hebes. There are many good forms but *Hebe* 'Margery Fish' is very hardy, free- and long-flowering with spikes of lavender flowers at the base. Still thinking of hardiness, the rosy red *Escallonia* 'C. F. Ball' is, I find, the least damaged by frost once it is established. It is wise, however, to protect young plants with sacking or bracken during bitter spells.

Most people know and admire the various forms of *Buddleia davidii* but not *Buddleia alternifolia*. It produces long arching branches festooned with lavender-purple flowers like ropes. It is seen to the best advantage when grown on a single stem about six feet high. Quite unlike any other members of the genus *Cytisus*, *C. battandieri* which comes from high in the Atlas Mountains is another choice small tree or shrub. Its trusses of golden flowers stand erect all along the branches. It is not a very long-lived tree – fifteen to twenty years perhaps – so it is wise to raise some seedlings every few years as replacements.

Viburnums need to be chosen with care. My favourite is *Viburnum tinus* 'Eve Price' which flowers profusely from January to April, the pink buds opening to white. It can be grown as a bush or as a useful hedge. Many fine plants have come from Rowallane and the form of *Viburnum tomentosum* that bears this name is in many ways a more useful shrub than the 'Lanarth variety'. It carries its flat heads of white flowers along horizontal branches in the same way as 'Lanarth variety', but it is a smaller neater plant which might fit better into an odd corner.

Unfortunately, the Rowallane variety of *Hypericum patulum* is not so hardy as *Hypericum* 'Hidcote', a superb shrub, or the newer 'Gold Cup'. These hypericums, with their large golden saucer-shaped flowers, are excellent for a shaded border or in full sun – and they respond well to a fairly hard pruning in spring if need be. For years *Philadelphus* 'Virginal' with its large double white flowers has been in the top flight of the mock oranges, but now it has given way to 'Enchantment'.

Jobs for March

IF March is kind and we are conscientious, we can catch up with work, and have the garden reasonably shipshape before the weekly chores of mowing and hoeing, planting, and spraying begin in April. Finish soil cultivations. Clear off weeds from herbaceous and shrub borders. Treat weeds under hedge bottoms or paths, among shrubs, fruit and bushes, with paraquat. Be prepared to give another treatment immediately if the persistent weeds show signs of life again. If you have couch grass treat it with dalapon.

Set about the lawn this month. Carefully remove stones, bones that the dog has forgotten, or odd toys that the children have left about, and sweep off worm casts before giving the lawn its first cut. If moss is present, kill it with a mercuric moss-killer, and do not bother to rake it out – it will soon disintegrate. But as I mentioned last month, a good scarifying with a wire rake, if there is a mat of old grass on the lawn, would do a power of good.

Make a resolution not to leave the lawn mowing for ten days or so. Mow the lawn lightly every five days if possible, setting the blades fairly high. If you use a push mower the work will be lighter. If you use a powered mower, remember the oftener you cut lightly, the less you cut off, and from a third to half the time spent cutting a lawn is taken in emptying the box and carting the mowings to the rubbish heap. And, far more important, light and frequent cutting makes for a lovely green lawn.

Prune winter-flowering jasmine by clipping back last year's shoots by about half their length. Prune hybrid tea and floribunda roses, gooseberries, and red currants.

Check all plants – trees and shrubs, perennials or alpines – planted in the autumn, and if they have been loosened by frost, tread them in again firmly.

Make the effort to order any plants intended for planting this spring. We have now only about six weeks when planting can be done leisurely. After mid-April we must water or mulch more assiduously.

If new stocks of dahlias or chrysanthemums are required, place the order now; later on it may not be possible to obtain the desired varieties.

Plant gladioli, anemones and ranunculus.

Sow sweet peas and other hardy annuals if conditions permit. Order pea sticks, bean poles, and other garden sundries.

Depending on the weather and the state of the ground, a start may be made with sowings of vegetables – carrots, onions, and an early round-seeded variety of peas, broad beans, lettuces, radishes,

Brussels sprouts, cabbages, savoys and broccoli. Plant potatoes at the end of the month.

In the fruit and vegetable plantations this is an important month. There is still time to plant the 'remontant' or perpetual strawberries to have a crop in the autumn. Also, one can plant in March all the soft fruits as well as apples and pears. Finish pruning this month, and give all fruits a dressing of a fruit fertiliser.

In the greenhouse, press on with sowings of stocks, antirrhinums, and other half-hardy annuals. Repot foliage plants that have outgrown their pots. Take cuttings of dahlias and chrysanthemums. Start begonia tubers into growth. Sow sweet peas outdoors, or in frames or under cloches.

Apply total weedkillers to paths and drives. And when using paraquat for weeds in beds and borders, or under hedges, take care not to allow the chemicals to touch the foliage of cultivated plants.

In the house, the foliage plants in pots will begin to perk up and grow now. Move them into a slightly less light spot – away from the full sun – wash the leaves to remove dust, and give them a liquid feed. Any that are now too large for their pots may be repotted in a compost such as John Innes or the peat-based 'Levington' compost.

April

The month of April usually lays down the pattern of the garden's success or failure. If it is kindly, warm, with frequent and gentle showers, the ground will warm up, plants will grow apace and the garden owners will be enticed into the garden, there to keep on top of the work. So too will the old folk and the handicapped, so it is worth studying the tools that will make their work easier. If Easter is fine this is an added bonus because in the four-day holiday the backlog of work can be eliminated, or at least greatly reduced.

The lawns cry out for attention; in greenhouses and frames there is much work to be done. As the ground warms later in the month one puts on mulching materials. Seeds may be sown. Pests appear, and have to be dealt with smartly. Fertilisers have to be applied. April is an exciting month with spring flowers opening daily, and the birds paying a little for their keep by their morning song. That is all true of a clement April; but an unkind one does not bear thinking about.

Choosing the right tool

IF you are buying a house and furnishing it you are unlikely to have much money left for equipping the garden with even the essential tools. They all have to be bought on a shoe string, and out of force of habit many people soldier on with old fashioned and perhaps cumbersome tools. But with advancing years it pays to review the toolshed and the advances that have been made in tool design and materials.

Unfortunately for tall people, the designers of tools are ever mindful of the fact that the average height of a British male is about 5 ft 9 in. and they design accordingly. Any physiotherapist will tell you that if you have to bend over to use a hoe or rake, or push a mower, you are putting strain on the back muscles before even doing any work at all. If you have to put cross strain on the muscles by the action of hoeing, obviously you will tire more easily.

It is essential when choosing hoes and rakes to make certain that they can be used in a standing-up position if at all possible. The length of handle is therefore very important and with the Wolf range of tools one can have a choice of three lengths. I have been trying one or two experiments myself, and I tentatively suggest the top of the handle, with the head resting on the ground, should just about come up to the lobe of one's ear.

When choosing a mowing machine, whether hand-propelled or power-driven, make sure that the handles are adjustable for height. This has been overlooked by some manufacturers, though it is an important refinement.

A detailed investigation into the needs of disabled people is now being carried out, and it is certain that as a result many modifications to existing tools will be made. It is certain, too, that modifications which make life easier for handicapped people will also make life easier for the able-bodied. The introduction of the

Wilkinson two-handed pruner is an excellent example. Mr H. B. Randolph, chairman of the Wilkinson Sword Company, is suffering from a touch of arthritis in his hands, and he found it difficult to prune his roses with an ordinary pair of secateurs. So he gave his design team the challenge, which they have met magnificently in the new two-handed pruner. This consists of the ordinary blade assembly of the well-known Sword pruner with 11 in. handles equipped with a well-moulded plastic grip. Thus one can attack a rose bush or any other bush without the hands coming anywhere near the thorns, and of course great pressure can be exerted with little effort. I must emphasise that this is not only a tool for handicapped people – parks departments in this country and in America are already placing large orders for it.

In all gardens there is the constant problem of moving quantities of soil, grass mowings, leaves and other rubbish, and the one-wheeled wheelbarrow is an anachronism today. One is still half carrying the load. But with the two-wheeled truck equipped with pram handle loads are moved with much less effort. It is better still if the two-wheeled truck has a detachable body that can be lifted off to tip the contents onto the heap.

More and more liquids are being sold in aerosol cans. It is of course an expensive way of buying chemicals, but it is time- and effort-saving, and in these do-it-yourself days economy of time and effort is important. Even more important is the convenience of an aerosol pack of, say, insecticide, because only too often one notices that there are aphis on the roses and quick action would prevent a serious build-up of the pest. It is not always convenient to mix up a messy spray and find the spraying machine, but an aphis born on Sunday can be a grandmother by Wednesday so a quick attack with an aerosol spray is a good answer.

As garden chemicals proliferate it was probably inevitable that some of the registered trade names of the various formulations should be rather similar and could cause confusion. An example, as one reader has pointed out, is Weedol, the remarkable weedkiller based on paraquat, which acts only on the green matter in leaves and stems and is inactivated when it touches the soil. It could be confused with Weedex which is based on simazine, and is also a total weedkiller but remains active in the soil for practically the whole season. The best answer is still to read the label carefully and thoroughly understand the uses of the various chemicals.

Pool margins

IN these days when the emphasis is on the economy of labour in the garden, it is perhaps provocative to suggest the creation of a bog garden, or even a boggy area. The constant moisture needed by the bog-loving plants is most encouraging to weeds and they are not so easily controlled in such a spot as in some other parts of the garden. But even a small area that can be kept moist gives us a chance to grow well many lovely plants that would be impossible or indifferently successful on normal soils.

Some years ago before the plastics industry came to our aid I made a number of informal pools in my rock garden using concrete and facing the top edges with the local Bargate stone to match the rock-garden stone. A small pump recirculates the water from the lowest to the topmost pool. But every winter we have trouble with ice forming and causing cracks, so that water is lost in the pumping process and very soon the lower pool is empty. We have resurfaced all the pools with concrete and have placed a ball valve cunningly hidden under our overhanging flat juniper in the lower pool so that if water is lost by leaks and evaporation the level of this pool is always maintained automatically. Now, of course, there are new sealing compounds and these we shall use in due course, but the cracks had to be cemented over first.

Nowadays, too, you can make excellent pools by just excavating the ground and lining it with the plastic sheeting sold for the purpose. The edges are camouflaged by stones or plants and by allowing the pool to overflow a boggy margin is easily created.

Alternatively there are now informal plastic pools of various shapes, depths, and sizes which are simply sunk in the ground and are easy to install. My own preference is for the stone-coloured type, although some people prefer the blue type.

Progress is being made in the design of small submersible electric pumps. One manufacturer, mindful of safety where electricity is concerned, is now offering a pump which operates from a transformer at only 50 volts. It is capable of discharging 350 gallons an hour and is powerful enough to pump water up over a small waterfall and at the same time work several fountains.

Apart from the pleasure of running water, the plantsman can obtain great enjoyment from the boggy pool margins. Here such plants as trollius, calthas and dwarf bullrushes can be accommodated. Astilbes can be given exactly the conditions they revel in and those glorious flat-petalled Japanese irises, lovely forms of *Iris kaempferi*, can be made happy. The primulas too will grow lush and handsome and probably seed themselves with abandon. Ferns and various mimulus will grow luxuriantly and, of course, if one has plenty of room the giant rhubarb, varieties of *Rheum* and the huge-leaved *Gunnera manicata*, although this often needs winter protection in the colder districts.

It must not be thought that a boggy margin is essential for many of the plants I have mentioned. In my own quick-draining garden on light soil we grow *Primula rosea, P. pulverulenta* and the Bartley hybrids, and I am sure could grow many more. But we have chosen a fairly shady spot for them and equipped it with its own large mist nozzle that covers an area about 8 ft in diameter. This we turn on assiduously several times a week from April onwards if the weather is dry. It is easier to allow a pool to overflow its margins and give the surrounding ground a really good soaking. When preparing such an area for planting, it pays to work in plenty of peat to increase its moisture-holding capacity.

It is often objected that pools encourage midges. This is true, but if one has plenty of ornamental fish in the pools they should be able to take care of this problem. They and a sufficiency of fresh-water snails should also be able to control the green algae that always appear in the water if it is exposed to sunlight. But one needs to have a fair number of fish.

If the pool surface is largely protected by the leaves of floating aquatics, such as water lilies, aponogetons, and others, the algae do not thrive so fast. But there will always be the need for some scavengers like the ram's horn snail, or the freshwater winkle, or water mussels. All these together with suitable oxygenating submerged aquatic plants are supplied by the water-garden specialists.

Pruning problems

NEXT time you are in Paris, spare an hour to visit the Jardin du Luxembourg. There is nothing quite comparable to it in Britain – more beautiful gardens certainly, but none where young and old enjoy themselves, play a variety of games, and this in the heart of the city. But the *pièce de résistance* of the garden is its collection of trained pear trees. These are quite old now, but they are a superb example of pruning, restricting the trees to various shapes – pyramids, goblets, and so on – while keeping them in a highly fruitful condition. It is an education to see these trees and to talk with the old chaps who do the pruning.

Many authors have written about pruning, some more easily comprehensible than others, but too often my friends tell me that when they take the book out to their fruit tree, the 'before' and 'after' pruning drawings in the book bear no resemblance to their trees.

I like the definition of pruning in the Royal Horticultural Society's *Dictionary of Gardening*: 'Pruning consists in the removal of any part of a tree or shrub, either stem, branches, or roots. The term might be extended to apply to all operations in gardening which entail the cutting away of part of a plant, for the general effect will be the same, viz. the direction of the energies of growth into channels desired by the cultivator.' A bit pompous perhaps, but pithy, and it reminds us that pruning stimulates growth. One sometimes tends to forget this, especially when a tree or shrub has been planted too near another, or too near a wall. We chop it back fairly severely, but this just encourages new growth. Probably the only answer is to remove it.

Pruning not only encourages vigorous growth but we have to prune so that growth is likely to be produced where it will make a shapely young shrub or tree. And, of course, we prune, in many cases, to promote the production of flowers on ornamental trees and shrubs, and fruit on fruit trees.

The pruning of fruit trees and bushes is, let us face it, a fairly complicated business. The Royal Horticultural Society's *Fruit Garden Displayed*, price 9s 6d post paid, is tremendously helpful. But I suggest that attendance at a pruning demonstration at the Royal Horticultural Society's gardens at Wisley, or at some demonstration organised by a local education committee, would be very helpful. For example, one has to learn to differentiate between what books call 'old wood' and 'new wood'. This is really important with ornamental plants. 'New wood' is simply those shoots produced during the growing season, say April to September. They are usually lighter coloured than other shoots, thinner, whippier. Once you have learnt to spot 'new wood', pruning flowering shrubs is not very difficult.

The next thing to learn, and any good book will tell you, is whether the shrubs flower on new or old wood. Obviously if a shrub is going to flower in the spring or early summer on shoots produced in the summer of last year, one does not go round pruning it before it flowers. But immediately flowering is over, whatever pruning is necessary should be done. Such shrubs as weigelas, flowering currants, and mock orange are examples of shrubs that need an annual tidying up, removing old flowering shoots to make way for the new ones.

We need to prune in early spring only those shrubs that make new growth to carry flowers in the summer – the obvious example is *Buddleia davidii* and its varieties. It can be cut back really hard;

cut last year's shoots so that only two or three inches remain at the base.

On the other hand, *Buddleia alternifolia* produces its gorgeous ropes of mauve flowers on old wood, so any trimming or shortening of the long arching stems should be done immediately after flowering. Incidentally, where this shrub is being grown on a single stem, 5–6 feet high as it should be, in a few years the weight of the head of branches can be considerable – especially when covered with snow. So a really stout stake is necessary and I would suggest reinforcing it with a forked stake at an angle, or a supporting stake tied at an angle near the top of the main stake.

Turning to the subject of pruning roses about which so much has been written: first, when to prune. I know I am inviting trouble, but I still think it safe to prune in warm districts at any time from November to March or early April, if the weather is reasonable. But in the north-east and the colder parts of the north delay pruning until late March or early April.

Some years ago a friend who grows vast quantities of shrubs, roses, and fruit trees for the trade, concluded that the best way to grow roses for ordinary garden decoration is to plant them really close, prune them hard every year, and feed them lavishly. This technique works like a charm. Plant ordinary varieties, medium strong growers, 18 in. apart each way, and strong growers, like 'Peace', 'Queen Elizabeth', 'Buccaneer', and so on, 24 in. apart. Then prune them to leave two or at most three buds on each stem, cutting to an outward-pointing bud or eye. There is a good coverage every summer of foliage and flowers.

But this hard pruning does call for generous feeding. After all, we are cutting off every year about 90 per cent of last year's growth, and this has to be replaced – and fast. So after pruning you need a good dressing of an organic rose fertiliser. Put it on at the rates recommended by the makers; if you have a rather light soil, as I have, give an additional dressing of $1\frac{1}{2}$ oz. of superphosphate to the square yard.

One day when I have nothing else to do, I will try to find out who Mr Tonks was. It was he who worked out the famous fertiliser

formula which is still very popular with rose growers. Some of my
rose books talk about his fertiliser, but do not get around to
Mr Tonks. You can buy it ready made, with I think one or two
refinements, or you can make it up yourself. This is the famous
Tonks formula: 12 oz. superphosphate, 10 oz. nitrate of potash,
2 oz. sulphate of magnesium, 1 oz. sulphate of iron, and 8 oz.
gypsum. This mixture is put on in April, well crushed up, at 4 oz.
to the square yard. I think the magnesium and the superphosphate
together have a powerful effect.

The old problem of wisteria keeps cropping up. Should you
prune it in winter as well as in summer? Personally I prune in
summer and leave it at that. But if you pinched back the new
growths in summer to leave only two or four leaves, you can, if
you wish, prune the spurs back in winter to leave two buds only.
I have never seen any good reason for doing this, and I have been
enjoying massive displays of wisteria on two successive houses for
over twenty years.

No *plant hospital*

MY father, when he retired after nearly fifty years of professional
gardening, once confided to me that as all his life he had had to
grow plants where his employers wanted them to grow, and where
very often the plants did not want to grow, he was, in his own
garden, going to run no plant hospital and no plant mortuary.
From the day he retired until the day he died he owned no spraying machine, and I think only once did he ever use a chemical
fertiliser – to perk up his sweet peas which were lagging behind in
a cold, late spring. Of course he was able to obtain in the country
plentiful supplies of farmyard dung.

He had a rooted aversion to plants with thorns, berberis and the
like. The only thorny plants he would permit in his garden were
roses. Personally I share his aversion to the berberis family, and
looking round my own garden I find that without having adopted

any deliberate policy, we are singularly free from thorny plants apart from the rose and gooseberries.

But it is when I think back to my father's attitude towards pests and diseases that I feel we should possibly rethink our planting programmes so that we can avoid pests and disease trouble wherever possible. It is always dangerous to suggest that this or that plant is immune from pest or disease damage. It may be so in a thousand gardens, but it may be susceptible somewhere else. One can look around, or sit back and think about the plants that have never shown any susceptibility to pests or disease, or one can attack the problem more positively and ruthlessly remove all plants that have caused trouble in this respect. Perhaps unconsciously I have tended to eliminate the trouble-making plants in my own garden.

In these days when the chemists have worked overtime to provide us with powerful and efficient insecticides or fungicides, we can, if we wish, grow successfully virtually all the plants that we may desire to have in our gardens. We make it a rule to go round every Tuesday with a spraying machine, spraying all those plants that may be affected by greenfly, blackfly, thrips or caterpillars. This usually means only the roses, lilies, the broad beans and the fruit bushes. We use a combined insecticide and fungicide, which deals with black spot and mildew. The lilies we do take great care of, because they can be really crippled by botrytis disease, and of course the aphis can affect them with virus disease, so we try to keep the greenfly under control.

But going back to my father's point of view, there are so many plants that we can grow in any garden that give no trouble. There are the winter-flowering heathers, virtually all rock plants because, apart from the early flowering *Alyssum saxatile*, which is always attacked by our fantail pigeons, I cannot think of any of our common rock plants that have required protective spraying. In the herbaceous borders the erigerons, sometimes the geums, are attacked by the cuckoo spit insect which produces frothy masses on the stems, but these are easily controlled with a B.H.C. spray. For the rest, we never think of taking out the sprayer.

Diseases are another problem. In a dry season many of our michaelmas daisies have become whitened with mildew. So we have hardened our hearts and thrown them out.

At this time of the year there may be daffodils in the garden which look very sickly, and there may be patches in the beds or borders where the tulips have not grown well. The daffodils may have been affected by eelworm, or some disease, and they should be removed and burnt now. It would also be wise not to replant daffodils in this situation for four or five years. So, too, with the tulips; the tulip fire disease can affect a bed, and here again it is better to refrain from growing tulips in this situation for a few years. Certainly one can spray tulips with a chemical that will control the disease, but the easy way out is to grow something else in their place.

Rust disease on hollyhocks is well known and I would always advise those gardeners who wish to grow hollyhocks to raise them from seed every two years rather than try to control the rust disease by regular spraying. Again, there are chemicals that will control the rust disease, but they have to be applied frequently when the hollyhocks have started to make growth in the spring.

Once we move into the greenhouses, or consider growing plants in frames, the incidence of pests and diseases becomes much more important, and indeed more difficult to control. Here it is necessary to be exceedingly watchful and to take action at the first sign of trouble. In the warm humid atmosphere of a greenhouse or frame, pests and diseases can fructify very fast, so constant vigilance is necessary. It may be necessary to spray or fumigate with the various insecticidal smoke cones that are now available, every week or ten days if a complete control is to be obtained.

For greenhouses I would recommend the installation of one of the electric vaporising units which can be obtained on a contract basis. The suppliers provide all the chemicals necessary as part of the contract, and if some particularly obstinate pest turns up, a telephone call will bring the representative equipped with different types of fumigant chemical which, at least in my own experience, will nearly always effect a complete control.

Easy watering

HAVING been expatriated for some years during the war, I believe it to be true that the Englishman, far from home, longs for Britain's impossible, unpredictable and infinitely varied climate. As gardeners we could wish that it might be a little more consistent, but then, if it were, gardening would lose much of its challenge.

Since L. P. Smith and Dr Penman evolved their theory of irrigation by calculation some years ago many farmers and commercial growers have realised the enormous benefits that can be obtained by irrigation sensibly applied in relation to the amount of rain that falls. Many gardeners, too, the older diehards excepted, have discovered that water applied at the right moment can make a tremendous difference to the success of the crops.

It is probably a waste of time trying to persuade a professional gardener over the age of fifty-five to irrigate the garden regularly and consistently. But experimental work done in recent years shows conclusively that water applied at just the right moment can be invaluable. If the weather is dry, and if, for example, peas are watered at the time the flowers are setting, and again when the peas in the pods are beginning to swell, the crop can be increased considerably. In Cornwall experimental work has shown that one watering of a crop of cauliflowers at the crucial moment has increased the yield in cash tenfold.

The old gardener will always object that if you start watering you have to keep on, but what does this matter if the results justify the cost of the irrigation? There is always some period, it may be the spring, the summer, or the autumn, when insufficient rain falls in different parts of Britain for optimum growth.

Over the years I have painstakingly laid permanent irrigation over the whole of my garden. We have experimented with many types of sprinklers that will water a square, a rectangle, or even a long border 50 ft × 5 ft. Indeed there is one sprinkler that can be so adjusted to water each of these different areas. We have now settled in many parts of the garden for a simple type of sprinkler, known familiarly as the 'flip-flap' which throws out two jets, fore and aft, and will cover a 90 ft circle, provided one has a water pressure of not less than 35 lb. to the square inch. We have some of these sprinklers mounted on 6 ft galvanised pipes to water the vegetable garden, and we have another which is sold already mounted on a small stand and which can be moved from one part of the garden to the other. This is known as the Rainjet and at about 60s it is very good value for money.

We also have a number of 'pop-up' watering devices laid in the lawns, which, as their name suggests, pop up when the water is turned on, irrigate the lawn, and then drop back below the lawn level when the water is turned off. Unfortunately some water companies prohibit the use of these sprinklers if they are connected permanently to the main. They fear that there is some danger of contamination of the mains water supply. However, a non-return valve has been produced, and it is to be hoped that this will satisfy the water companies as to the safety of these permanent irrigation devices.

I am often asked whether I can justify the cost of irrigating my $2\frac{1}{2}$ acres? In a dry year I use about 200,000 gallons, which cost me about £25. In a normal year I would use only half that amount, and I am quite certain that this expenditure on water is economic, not only because of the good yields I get from my fruit and vegetables but because aesthetically the garden greatly benefits.

But being a Scotsman I go to considerable lengths to conserve moisture in the soil. We are conscientious about weed control because if the weeds are killed before they have made any appreciable amount of growth they have not had time to rob the ground of precious moisture. Then I am a great believer in the mulch. I use old mushroom-bed material from mushroom farms, peat, sawdust, spent hops, and if I was near a source of bracken I would use dried bracken applied thickly among my shrub borders, always for the same reason – the conservation of moisture and the suppression of weeds. Too few gardeners have really appreciated the value of a mulch. Not everybody lives near enough to a brewery to be able to obtain spent hops cheaply, but in most places sawdust can be bought at a reasonable price, and if this is applied, say 2 in. deep with a handful of sulphate of ammonia scattered over the mulch, it can save many weary hours of hoeing, and will help the plants enormously because it reduces evaporation of moisture from the soil.

Help for the handicapped

FOR some years I have been connected with an investigation into the problems of handicapped people in the garden. Perhaps one person in seven suffers from some disability, and old age in itself is a handicap when it comes to gardening. So the aids and techniques that help the disabled are in the main all tremendously helpful to the elderly. For me it has been an infinitely rewarding study. At the outset, several severely handicapped people – victims of poliomyelitis condemned to life in wheelchairs – came to my garden, and we brought out all the tools we thought they might be able to use. We sent them off round the garden to hoe, to dead-head roses, or to do half a dozen other jobs. It was most moving to hear the cries of delight when one of them called out: 'Yes. Come and see, I can do it! I can use it!'

The courage of handicapped people and their persistence never fail to move me greatly. What is even more appealing is that handicapped people who have been rehabilitated as far as their disability allows, go back to hospitals like the Nuffield Orthopaedic Centre, Oxford, to encourage patients there and show how their disability can be overcome.

At the outset we did not know what height a raised garden bed should be for a person in a wheelchair. We did not know how wide the bed should be, either for a wheelchair person, or for somebody who had to walk with a stick or a crutch. All these measurements have been established. We did not know, for example, what kind of paving to put down in a garden which would be safe for a person who walked with a rubber-shod walking stick.

The greenhouse is obviously a wonderful diversion for the housebound man. It is warm in the winter, and the handicapped owner can go into the greenhouse and work away happily at any time. But for somebody in a wheelchair opening the door is a problem, so manufacturers have made sliding doors for greenhouses. Then there was the problem of ventilation. The electric extractor fan, coupled with a thermostat, takes care of that. Shading the greenhouse is another problem, but we now have green plastic blinds which can be fitted inside the greenhouse. The string that operates them can be brought down underneath the bench so that raising or lowering the blinds is no trouble, even to a person in a wheelchair.

Manufacturers of garden tools and equipment have been wonderfully co-operative. Wilkinson Sword in particular have modified tools, and have produced hoes and long-handled small forks for pricking up the soil. They are adjustable for length, which is an important advance. Not only handicapped people will benefit from these adjustable tools – even the able-bodied need tools with handles of the right length for their particular height.

A great boon for the elderly or those unable to stoop is the Baronet long-handled weed puller. It is excellent for removing weeds from beds and borders. It is 31 in. long and has a trigger handle which operates the mechanism that grips the weed firmly enough to allow the user to pull it out of the ground.

Many handicapped people can use only one hand, so one-handed tools are a godsend. The Greensleeves one-handed trimmer enables the handicapped to snip off dead heads, trim hedges, and do many other jobs. So, too, with sprayers. There are now several sprayers on the market which can be pumped up and pressurised, then operated by a one-handed person.

Anyone who has to walk with a stick cannot manage a two-handled barrow, but the Portax and the Joyride trucks which have a pram handle are easily operated with one hand. Gathering weeds or fallen leaves is easy enough for the hale and hearty, but difficult for those who cannot bend or stoop. For them the Anita Garden Grab is the solution.

My garden is open to the public on behalf of the gardeners' charities on the last Sunday in June. For a couple of weeks before the great day we all try to polish up the place. My wife's aunt, who is now 93, loves to help in this great effort. For her we have a long-handled flower gatherer. This is a tool which cuts off the dead flowers, grips them, and brings them back to her left hand to be put in her basket. With this tool she does not have to penetrate into the rose bed or border, where she would probably get caught on the thorns, because the tool is 2 ft 6 in. long, and she can walk round the beds and borders without becoming entangled.

Research into the problems of disabled people in the garden still goes on. Eventually a manual will be published for those concerned with the rehabilitation of the disabled, and I am certain it will be of great interest to many other people as well. While we wait for the publication, those interested in this problem can obtain from the Disabled Living Activities Group of the Central Council for the Disabled, 39 Victoria Street, London, S.W.1, a booklet entitled *Gardening for the Disabled* (1s post paid), which contains useful hints and suggestions. There are also tool lists, plans and instructions for making raised beds and raised frames – the complete set for 2s postage included.

Modern tools and machines have made life much easier for handicapped people. As a gardener, I am keenly interested in the types of plants that handicapped people should grow. When the gardening manual for handicapped people does appear, it will contain not only advice about machines, tools and equipment, but much information about plants that will suppress weeds and which need the minimum of attention. Obviously, as far as possible, they should grow plants that smother weeds so that hoeing and weeding are eliminated. They should plant herbaceous plants that need no staking, and there are many to choose from. They may wish to grow fruit – apples and pears. Obviously, tall standard trees are out of the question, but they can grow apples on the Bouché Thomas system which, broadly speaking, is a fruit hedge about 4 ft high. Or they can grow red currants and gooseberries as upright cordons to a height of about 4 ft.

Mrs Frances Perry, the horticultural adviser, was called in to give some advice at a convent, and the Mother Superior said she would like to have a fruit hedge, like that which she had seen at the mother convent in France. This turned out to be a system of fruit growing devised by a M. Bouché Thomas, and it has proved very easy to manage and particularly suitable for disabled or handicapped people.

For this purpose one can use trees of apple and pear, three, four, five or even six years old. Very often it is possible to buy fruit trees quite cheaply from nurserymen, because it always happens that a certain number may have started off as cordons, or dwarf bush trees, and have not made very shapely specimens. However, they are perfectly satisfactory for making a hedge.

They should be planted in a row about 6 ft apart, and it is important to plant them about one foot deeper than one would normally plant fruit trees. By doing this, the lower branches are almost at ground level. Then posts are put in at each end of the row, and three wires are stretched between them, about 18 in. apart, the lowest wire being about 18 in. above the ground.

Some people fear that this deep planting may encourage scion-rooting, and unwanted vigour in later years. Frances Perry did not find that this happened, but I suppose it could do so with some varieties. Mr Geoffrey Ellis considers that apples worked on MM 106, MM 111, M 1X or MV 11A rootstocks are good for hedges. The system is being increasingly used by commercial fruit growers, and some of them stretch only one wire between posts as a support. Recommended varieties include Cox's Orange Pippin, Laxton's Superb, George Cave, Grenadier and Lord Lambourne.

As the trees grow, all the shoots pointing forwards or backwards are removed, and those pointing sideways are tied to the wires.

Thus in a very short time, a fairly compact hedge of shoots is produced. It may be necessary to do some pruning here and there to persuade the branches to produce side shoots that will fill in bare patches. However, after that, very little pruning is required beyond cutting out the shoots that point forwards or backwards. One can do this pruning in summer or winter. The hedge may be kept pruned to about 4 or 5 ft high, as desired.

It is a very simple way of growing fruit, and these hedges are quite ornamental. If one wishes to screen an eyesore or to make a division between the ornamental and utilitarian part of the garden, a fruit hedge is both attractive and productive. For people who are partially disabled, and especially for blind people, this is an excellent method. The blind find it is particularly easy to handle, because if the young shoots pointing forwards or backwards are removed when they are soft, there is no danger of the blind person walking into protruding branches.

Also very suitable for the small garden, and for handicapped people, are red or white currants and gooseberries grown as upright cordons. This is really quite simple. Bushes are planted about one yard apart in a line. Again posts are fixed at each end of the row, and a wire stretched between them at about 4 ft above ground. Bamboo canes are then inserted three to each plant, one immediately behind the plant, and the other two about one foot on either side and tied to the wire. Another bamboo cane is tied to the upright canes horizontally about one foot above ground.

As the bushes produce shoots, three are selected, one growing vertically upright, and two others which are so placed that they can be carefully bent down and tied to the lower cane. All others are removed. Then, as the shoots grow, the middle one is tied to its cane and the two side branches are tied first to the horizontal cane and then gently bent round to the vertical position. In a year or two the shoots will have reached the top of the cane, and the top growth can be pinched out. Side shoots will, of course, form and these are summer-pruned by pinching them back, and if necessary pruned a bit harder in winter. With gooseberries, I always prefer to leave the final pruning until spring, and it may be necessary in bird-infested districts to protect the buds with netting or Scaraweb. One can allow these cordons to grow much higher than 4 ft, of course, but for easy handling 4 ft to 6 ft would be about right. Again, there is a triple purpose in having these fruit bushes grown as vertical cordons – they make an excellent screen, are easy to handle, and quite productive.

More interesting is the production of standard red or white currants. A cutting about one foot long is taken in the autumn when the leaves have fallen, and inserted in the ground in the open garden to about half its depth. The base of the cutting will callus over and root in the spring. Each plant needs a stake, and the leading shoot tied to it as it grows. Side shoots should be pinched back in the summer but not removed entirely because the leaves are needed for the continued growth of the plant.

In a year or two the cutting will have grown to 3 or 4 ft, and the top is then pinched out. This encourages the production of side branches near the top of the stem, and these are pinched back in summer to encourage even more side branches. When there is a sufficient head of branches at the top of the stem, all side branches down the stem are removed, leaving it quite clean.

One advantage of growing red and white currants as standards is that other crops can be grown beneath them. They are excellent for a fruit cage and I know many people who live in gardens where there is a superabundance of birds, who have to grow not only their fruit, but peas and even cabbages in the fruit cage. Dwarf peas can be grown under standard red or white currants quite easily.

Gooseberries may also be grown as standards, but here it is not feasible for the amateur to grow his own. Standard gooseberries are grafted upon a rootstock of the flowering currant *Ribes aureum*. Again, one can grow other crops beneath them.

Jobs for April

IN the flower beds and borders, lose no time now hoeing off weeds, cutting down old dead stems, and tidying up the decayed leaves of plants. About the middle of the month in the south, and a bit later in the north, mulch all these borders and beds if possible with peat, sawdust, mushroom compost, or any similar material.

If the lawns have not been given their spring treatment, this should be done now – as far as possible within one's limitations of time and labour. Scarify with a wire rake, true up the edges, and if not already done, apply a good lawn fertiliser.

Check ties on all climbing roses, wistarias and the like against walls or fences, and ties keeping newly planted trees to their stakes. As soon as the leaves appear, the extra weight, together with a heavy downpour of rain, may prove the last straw for semi-rotten ties. Plastic-covered wire is excellent for securing climbing roses and the like to supports, but always leave sufficient room around the stems for them to swell without any danger of the wire cutting into the bark.

All pruning should be finished by now, but if roses, *Buddleia davidii*, forsythias, and winter jasmines have not been pruned, then this should be done.

There is still time to plant gladioli and corms of ranunculus and anemones. Old dahlia tubers may be planted out towards the end of the month, but if the stems appear above ground and there is danger of night frost, be prepared to cover them with newspapers, or draw some soil over them.

In the vegetable plot, sowings of peas, broad beans, carrots, lettuces, beetroot, may be made, and if not already done, savoys, Brussels sprouts, sprouting broccoli, and similar vegetables for autumn and winter may be sown on a prepared seed bed for transplanting later on.

Make sure there are some pea sticks available for autumn-sown peas, and indeed for that matter peas that may have been sown in March.

In the greenhouse, seeds may be sown now of such half-hardy annuals as zinnias and asters. In cold greenhouses tomato plants may be put in towards the middle of the month in the milder districts, but later in the colder parts of the country.

Be vigilant, because pests are very active at this time of year. Caterpillars on gooseberries and roses, aphis on all the plants that are susceptible to this pest are on the move. Take a walk round the garden once or twice a week just looking for trouble, and keep a plentiful supply of the appropriate insecticides handy. Take action as soon as there is the slightest sign of trouble, and repeat the spray about every seven to ten days. Watch strawberries particularly, as aphis can easily be working away unobserved down in the crowns of the plants.

May

Depending on where we live, May is the month when we can throw off the restraints of the threat of frost, bed out the summer flowers, turn the heat off in the greenhouse, and get out the garden furniture. In the south and in the home counties we can hope to see the last of the frosts in the third week of May. In the north, probably they may continue into early June. So it pays to listen to the forecasts and take evasive action if required.

Watering and feeding are important now – both with indoor plants, in the greenhouse and in the open garden. Increased vigilance regarding the incidence of pests and disease; going round the garden with a 'seeing eye', staking plants in good time – this is the order of the day for the merry month of May.

Weed and feed

No garden owner, no matter how inexperienced, will expect to take a cabbage crop off his vegetable plot year after year without returning some kind of manure or fertiliser to the soil. Yet I know many intelligent people who cheerfully take off the equivalent of two or three hay crops from their lawns ever year but never think of applying any fertiliser.

Then they become mildy aggrieved when the inevitable happens – the grass becomes poor, and moss begins to make its appearance. Let me hasten to add that the poverty of the turf alone is not in some cases the cause of the moss taking hold. It can and does appear in lawns that have been regularly fertilised, and even on lawns that are very swiftly drained, such as my own. However, today the moss problem is swiftly dealt with by the mercuric moss-killers. These not only destroy the moss, but they also control the spores for a long time, thus preventing a secondary infestation by the moss. When moss is killed by mercuric chemicals there is no need to rake it out if you do not wish to.

Returning to the question of lawn fertilisers, much research has been done in recent years not only on the balance of the chemical content, but on the types of chemical used, and on the carriers that are employed to make spreading of the chemical easy. We have long been familiar with the so-called 'weed and feed' fertilisers which contain a small amount of selective weedkiller, and effectively control weeds and fertilise the turf at the same time. More recently we have seen the Hi-lite fertilisers based upon peat, such as Evergreen 80, and as they are concentrated and exceedingly light; a given area of lawn can be treated with about a quarter of the weight of fertiliser that would have been required if the older types were used. Nowadays all fertilisers are so formulated that they can be applied through different types of fertiliser spreader, and these are really most useful tools.

If there have been any problems in the lawn, such as moss, poor growth, the invasion of clover or other difficult weeds, it would be worth while taking some advice, and possibly sending a sample of the soil off for a lime test. Alternatively, you can buy quite cheaply a reasonably efficient lime-testing kit which enables you to do the test at home and ascertain the pH, that is the measurement of the amount of lime in the soil.

Writers of books on lawns are, understandably, rather reticent about recommending a level of pH. The pH of the soil is only one among many factors that determine the growth of the grass, but it is generally accepted here and in America that the finer grasses grow best in a slightly acid soil, that is a soil with a pH of between 6 and 6·5. Where clover is spreading, this probably means that the lawn is on the alkaline side; this will also encourage the proliferation of worms, and attempts should be made to reduce the alkalinity by the application of sulphate of ammonia or some similar fertiliser. On the other hand, continued application of such fertilisers on naturally acid soils could make the soil too acid to produce good turf. In such cases it is desirable to dress the lawn with Nitrochalk at the rate of, say, ½ oz. to the square yard and to water this fertiliser well in. One or two dressings at this rate may be given during the growing season.

Manufacturers of many fertilisers state that it is not necessary to water them in, and under normal conditions this is probably accurate. On the other hand there are freak conditions from time to time when damage may be caused, and in any case I always prefer to water my fertilisers in immediately after they have been applied, because not only does this eliminate any risk of burning, but it helps to get the fertiliser down to the roots more quickly. Incidentally, one of the small slitting machines that are on the market today, run over the lawn before the fertiliser is applied, helps enormously to allow water and fertiliser to penetrate quickly to the roots.

Turning to the use of fertilisers in their wider applications, it is useful to consider their effect. Because the tomato is such an important crop much concentrated work has been done on the feeding of tomatoes under glass, and the findings are broadly applicable to plants of all kinds, whether grown under glass or in the open. Briefly, one should fertilise according to the weather. To take the tomato as the classic example, a week or so of bright sunshine has the same effect upon the plants as a large dose of potash fertiliser. So to correct this it is normal to apply a quick-acting nitrogenous fertiliser, such as soluble dried blood at the rate of about $\frac{1}{2}$ oz. to the plant, well watered in or dissolved in water. Conversely, a period of dull weather affects the plants in the same way as an overdose of nitrogen would – they become lush, soft, and spindly, and in order to bring them into balance again an application of a potash fertiliser is needed. Here about $\frac{1}{4}$ to $\frac{1}{2}$ oz. of sulphate of potash for each plant, again well watered in, is the answer.

It is more difficult, of course, to apply this sort of fertilising technique with plants growing in the open, but the principles are the same. You should be prepared to ring the changes depending upon the type of summer we have. If, for example, the summer is predominantly hot and dry, then either fertilisers with a heavy nitrogen bias can be used, or supplementary applications of nitrogen should be given over and above the dressings of the normal balanced plant food which one is in the habit of using. Similarly, if the summer should be dull, occasional applications of potash to the crops would be helpful.

While many people accept the need for applying fertilisers to quick-growing crops such as vegetables and the lawn, they are less generous with their treatment of fruit trees and bushes. But it must be remembered that between now and the end of August our fruit trees and bushes will not only have to make the growth for next year's crops, but that some time probably in July the weather and our treatment of the plants will decide what kind of yield they are likely to give next year. That is the time when fruit bud formation is decided. So a good dressing of a general fruit fertiliser applied according to the makers' instructions now, generous mulching with any kind of mulch material that is available, plentiful watering in dry weather – all these treatments will pay a handsome dividend next year.

This applies also to shrubs, especially those that have been planted in recent years; water them in dry weather, and a reasonable application of organic fertiliser will be much appreciated, and the shrubs will reward us with plentiful growth.

Coping with pot plants

IT is probably true to say that more plants indoors are killed by overwatering than by neglect in this respect. One of the villains of the piece is the 'cache-pot' – the pottery receptacle which is not equipped with a drainage hole, into which you put the ordinary clay pot to make it more attractive in the living room.

Too often pot plants in these cache-pots are watered, the excess drains through into the cache-pot and after several waterings it is quite possible that a good half-inch of water has built up there unnoticed. No plant really likes to be sitting in half an inch of water and some plants resent it very quickly. If you have plants in cache-pots lift the pot out every week or so to make quite sure there is no surplus pool of water at the bottom. Similarly, when plants are being grown in pots standing on a saucer, if the soil in the pot does not immediately absorb any surplus water that has run into the saucer – say within an hour or so – then the saucer should be emptied.

This brings me to the subject of watering plants in a greenhouse. Much attention has been given by manufacturers in recent years to the problem of automatic watering in greenhouses and there is no doubt that the sub-irrigation systems that are now available work extremely well. Basically these consist of equipment that will keep a layer of sand on a greenhouse bench constantly moist so that the pot plants can draw up what they require from

the wet sand by capillary attraction. Installation of one of these
devices is not difficult, provided, of course, one has a source of
mains water supply laid on to the greenhouse.

If plants are being grown in clay pots one has to modify the
potting technique a little for sub-irrigation. The crock normally
used to cover the hole in the pot is removed and replaced with
about an inch of peat. Then it is necessary to give the pots a firm
twist and shove into the sand to make quite certain that the wet
sand is making contact with the peat in the bottom of the pot.
After that the water will rise by capillary attraction and the plants
will take up what they need and no more.

With plastic pots, of course, you do not put crocks in the
bottom, and all that is necessary is to make quite certain that the
wet sand is in contact with the soil through the holes in the bottom
of the plastic pots.

It is remarkable how plastic pots have swept into favour, both
with·commercial growers and with the amateur. It is only a few
years ago that I wrote enthusiastically about plastic pots and was
assailed on all sides by growers who were certain that the plants
would never grow as well in plastic as in a clay pot. Prices have
come down smartly.

There is no need for me to elaborate upon the advantages of
plastic pots – they are light to handle, easy to clean and they do not
seem to gather algae as do the clay pots. Handled carefully, they
will last for many years and plants grow well in them. It must be
remembered that plants need rather less watering in a plastic
pot than they do in a clay pot. The reason, of course, is that a clay
pot will evaporate moisture through its sides, whereas a plastic
pot does not. So it is important not to mix clay and plastic pots
in a batch of plants. Keep them separate so that the plants in plastic
do not run into any danger of being overwatered.

One large grower has told me that he has been able to produce
plants just as well in plastic pots as in clay pots, with the single
exception of the cyclamen. For some reason that has not yet been
discovered he finds that his cyclamen still grow better in a clay pot.
Not that the cyclamen in plastic pots are to be despised; I grow

very passable cyclamen in plastic pots myself and as I am not trying to produce show specimens I am quite content.

Foxing the birds and the squirrels

ONCE I took a party of Danish gardeners round the garden, and I was most amused to hear their comments about birds. Apparently birds in Denmark are as big a problem in the garden as they are to us, but they have the same attitude to birds as we do. As one lady said, 'If a blackbird gets caught in the strawberry net, we just go and let him out.' This, of course, completely contrasts with the attitude of the French who, with their inescapable logic, treat them as pests, and control them by shooting.

However, the new lightweight nylon netting is proving an enormous help in protecting fruits like raspberries and strawberries. It is so light and there is no need to rig a massive framework to drape it over. By using the rubber Hortiballs into which bamboo canes can be pushed to make a framework, an adequate covering can be erected quickly. One advantage of these rubber Hortiballs is that the net is easily draped over the bamboo framework and does not catch on corners.

As anyone who has tried to net a fruit plot knows, a blackbird will use great ingenuity to find a way in, and it is important to fix the net down firmly by laying pieces of old water pipe, or something similar, on it. Squirrels, too, will bite their way through the net, and they can be most exasperating. One friend of mine has overcome the squirrel problem by erecting a metal fruit cage with wire netting sides and a nylon net on top. He mounted on insulators just above the top framework a wire coupled to an electric fencing unit as used by farmers. When the squirrels climbed the wire netting to bite through the nylon, they touched the electric fence and soon learnt to give the cage a wide berth.

A bouquet from America

ONCE I published a letter from an American lady who wanted to be put in touch with correspondents in this country. Here is the delightful letter she sent me some months afterwards:

Where are those legendary reserved English women? You know – the tweed-skirted gal, trowel in hand, hair in a bun, that will not communicate with strangers. The one that prefers the company of her faithful horse or dog to people! I know where they are – they are residing in the imagination of Hollywood fiction writers.

Since a portion of my letter was printed in your column, requesting Englishwomen interested in gardening as a correspondent – I have been deluged with the most fascinating mail. Every letter from a unique and charming lady, each one offering friendship, seeds, catalogues, and exchange of mutual interests. I have been able to sit in my living room and share the joys of your English springtime. The delight of the fruit trees in blossom, woodlands filled with primroses, and the meadows golden with daffodils, the promise of riotous colour this summer will bring. I have shared the enthusiasm of gardeners who delight in growing the unusual plant on wide windowsills and in home greenhouses. I have 'oohed' and 'aahed' at anyone living in a house 500 years old and restoring its garden. I have shared the loss of a pet swan, and smiled at the return of the swallows. I have clucked in disgust at snails chomping at delphiniums (how dare they?) and developed blisters mentally, helping a woman restore a herb garden. What pleasure to share the satisfaction of children making good progress in school, and smile with their mothers over their talents and creativity. I've travelled abroad with these ladies and have visited Wales, Ireland, India, Spain, Greece, Denmark, and even took a tour of my own United States. All from my living room.

I have even done a bit of worrying. You know – polluted rivers, country lands and villages being ravished by the population explosion. I, too, worry about morality, famine, Vietnam and black rebellions.

When the day comes that I have the money to make a trip to England I shall not feel like a foreigner on strange and alien soil; I will feel more like an English daughter that has been gone for a long time and returned to visit her people. I am proud to be an American housewife and mother. I love my country, and hold my freedom dear – however I am very proud that my ancestors were British pioneers. Those hard working and courageous people of the 1600s and 1700s are the backbone of our country. American patriots – Washington, Henry, Madison, Monroe, Jefferson – all English.

I would not doubt for a moment that when one of my ancient grandmothers got off the boat in Jamestown, Virginia, she had packets of her favourite flower seeds tucked away in her apron pocket.

Thank you for your consideration.
Most sincere best wishes.
BILLIE BARKER.

Mrs. Quinton T. Barker,
10902 Mc. St.,
Anaheim, California.

Thoughts about tubs

THIS is just about the trickiest period for a gardening journalist in the whole year. The average date of the last frost can vary by about three weeks in different parts of Britain, and in our ridiculous climate even that date can, in about one year in five or six, be wildly out. I am still smarting over the frost we had in the last few days of May several years ago. Readers in the north will no doubt smile a trifle wryly about this as they can suffer frosts in June and indeed as early as August.

However, one has to take a few risks in gardening, and in the southern half of England it should be safe now to plant out the summer bedding, and deck out our window boxes, hanging baskets, tubs and the like with begonias, fuchsias, geraniums, and the rest.

In smart town courtyards and on the terraces of neat Georgian houses, teak or oak tubs are called for, but in less formal surroundings an old beer barrel cut in half answers very well. We have just acquired a couple through the good offices of our local wine merchant, cut them in half, treated the woodwork with dark-coloured Cuprinol, and painted the metal bands first with rustproofing fluid, and then with a coat of black paint. These metal bands are really the most vulnerable part of the tub. By the way, never use creosote on tubs, fences, posts or pergolas, or anywhere near growing plants.

I mention old beer barrels because I have an idea that with the increasing use of metal beer casks, they may soon be collector's pieces. A neighbour acquired with his house some fourteen years ago a magnificent wooden water butt, about four feet high. It is now on its last legs, and he is resigning himself to buying a 40-gallon plastic butt complete with tap for about £5 carriage paid.

One might ask why anybody should bother to collect rainwater, apart from using it to wash hair. I do not like rainwater tanks in a greenhouse. It is almost impossible to keep them free from contamination, and research has shown that it is better to put on cold pure water direct from the tap than to use warm water – disease soup, as one scientist once described it to me – from a rainwater tank. But the water butt can be very useful if we should run into a dry summer and garden water is prohibited. After all, with a little ingenuity one can often conduct the bath water into the butt, and this reserve supply may make the difference between life and death to trees or shrubs planted rather late in the spring.

Returning for a moment to tubs, window boxes, and similar containers, I am surprised that so few people make use of horticultural vermiculite. A good thick layer of this material – say the bottom third of the container – will retain ten times its weight of moisture and greatly reduce the frequency of waterings.

Jobs for May

IN the south and home counties, to play safe do not plant out tender plants – tomatoes, zinnias, geraniums, and the like, until about May 20. Further north, wait until the first week of June.

As soon as spring bedding plants – wallflowers, myosotis and the rest – are over, clear the beds and take time to work in plenty of manure, compost, hop manure, or some other good organic plant food. It is better to do this now than in the autumn. The dressing will leave enough food in the soil for next year's spring bedding plants.

Continue to spray roses and other plants liable to be infested with greenfly. Use a combined spray or dust for the lilies – one that contains an insecticide and a fungicide.

Plant out summer cabbages, cauliflowers, and other brassicas raised under glass.

Sow sweet corn and marrows, French and runner beans, towards the middle of the month. Continue to sow successional crops of salads and peas.

Lay lifted tulips in a trench to ripen off the bulbs. Put a length of wire netting in the trench, lay the bulbs on this and cover with soil. Then when the tops have died down, the bulbs are easily lifted and none are left in the trench.

Stake delphiniums and other herbaceous plants. Lift and divide polyanthus and primroses after flowering. Sow seeds of cheiranthus, wallflowers, myosotis, hollyhocks, sweet williams, and the like for flowering next year.

On lawns, slash coarse grasses with a sharp knife repeatedly to weaken them and give the finer grasses a chance to take over.

Water weeds in the turf with a selective weedkiller, using a fine rose or a sprinkle bar on the can.

If you have taken over a new garden and it is rather empty, a cheap way of filling parts of it is to raise hardy perennials from seed. Many of them may be sown now in pots or boxes, outdoors in a shady place, and in a couple of years will make a fine show. Lupins, delphiniums, phloxes, oriental poppies, *Gypsophila paniculata*, and many more are easily raised from seed. The seedlings may vary a bit, and one may discard any that are not very exciting, but on the whole they come very true from seed.

June

If ever we are to have time to sit and admire the results of our labours it should be in June, July, and August. True, the weeds will flourish in direct proportion to the productivity of the garden, and pests will fructify, but in general, June should be a kind month with no major tasks to undertake and warm enough to tempt the old folks out to do a little gentle gardening. At this time the children will be more likely to enter into the fun of the garden than if they are asked to help in the less inviting months.

Admittedly we have the 'June gap' when vegetables are scarce and we are anxiously awaiting the first of the strawberries. But the flowers of summer are coming along fast now and almost before we realise it, the longest day will have come and gone. Then we shall begin the long slow slide into autumn and winter. So make the most of June.

The problems of shade

In Scotland we have a saying that nothing flourishes under fir trees or factors, the Scots term for an estate manager. This is another way of saying that the best fertiliser is the farmer's footprints. But even if he perambulates regularly all round his domain there are places under the trees where it is difficult to establish any ground cover. Thankfully I have no fir trees, but I have a sycamore, and I now despair of getting anything to grow beneath it. Daffodils certainly survive, but nothing else that we have tried. I thought I had found the answer when I foolishly planted out my whole stock of the dwarf chamomile that never produces a flower stem, the variety known as 'Treneague'. As it grows right up to the trunks of the trees in Buckingham Palace gardens, I assumed that chamomile would put up with lodging beneath the sycamore. Unfortunately I lost the lot during its first autumn and winter.

The problem of growing plants under trees is complicated. First of all, some plants do not like the drip of moisture from the trees above them; then it is usually dry under trees, but not always. The easy way out is to settle for bulbs – snowdrops, crocuses, and daffodils – allow the native grasses to grow if they will and leave it at that.

This is rather defeatist, and one should look at the few plants that will put up with the drip of other trees. The snowberry, varieties of *Symphoricarpus* which, while perhaps not very exciting, does have white berries in the autumn; the two species of *Rubus*, *R. nutkanus* and *R. odoratus*; cotoneasters and box can be brought into use in such a position, as can the various berberis, *Mahonia bealei*, and that rather scarce plant nowadays, *Pachysandra*. Why the *Pachysandra* has not become more popular in this country I cannot imagine, as it is used widely both on the Continent and in the

United States. It covers the ground with a beautiful green carpet about a foot high; it spreads rapidly, can be propagated with ease, and will grow under the densest shade, under the canopy of large trees that shield it from all but the heaviest of downpours. The *Aucuba*, even if it has nothing else to commend it in many eyes, will again put up with the drip of trees.

Plants for reasonably normal shade, where the ground is not too dry, are fairly plentiful. Some people acquire, or inherit, these problem spots in gardens, but in almost any garden after a few years when trees have been planted and begun to mature, the problem presents itself. In my own garden there is little enough in the way of shade, apart from the sycamore, an enormous Bramley apple, and a truly magnificent *Prunus subhirtella*. The first year of our occupancy the *Prunus* flowered magnificently, but in the following autumn the market-gardener neighbour removed all his hedges and the birds removed themselves into my garden. Since the tree is about 30 ft high, it is impossible to do anything in the way of protecting the buds in winter, and we have never seen a blossom on it for the past twelve years.

In these shaded spots we find the hostas do exceedingly well – all the varieties, both green and variegated, although their leaves are very often painfully ragged through the depredations of slugs and snails. Then in another border alongside these trees, and shaded on the south side by the house, we find practically the whole range of herbs will do quite well. It would never have occurred to me to plant a herb border in almost total shade – we are accustomed to seeing them out in the full sun. No doubt they would have done much better had they had more sunlight, but as this border was the nearest spot we could find to the kitchen, that is where they had to go. It is a raised border on top of a flat stone wall, which dries out quickly. If the water pressure is good one of the 'flip-flap' sprinklers, which covers a good 90 ft circle, just reaches it.

But we have thyme, balm, rue, fennel, two kinds of mint (the ordinary dark-leaved variety and the apple mint which some people aver is the only kind to use for mint sauce), and tansy. Others, I am sure, would put up with such a position, especially if we could be bothered to arrange more regular watering in dry spells.

The prostrate junipers, the savin or *Juniperus sabina*, and *J. horizontalis*, have done remarkably well under heavy shade, and I have been surprised to find that some of the old-fashioned shrub roses have performed very creditably under the shade of a large laburnum. Of course with a little attention to mulching, ground preparation, incorporating plenty of peat, and a fixed watering point that can be turned on whenever necessary, one can grow many desirable plants under shade.

It may be objected that as there are so many plants that will grow in any garden it is foolish to go to all this trouble, but I am prepared to go to a good deal of trouble to have a few Candelabra primulas, some *Meconopsis betonicifolia* 'Bailey's variety' – the blue poppies – and other woodland gems. It is surprising what can be done now that we have that gardeners' boon, Alkathene pipe. This semi-rigid plastic pipe is easily punctured with a bradawl filed down to about the size of a gramophone needle, and if buried just under the ground, can be used to flood a small area to grow the bog-loving plants. Curiously enough, the holes, even if the pipe is buried in the soil, do not seem to clog up, but if it was found that not enough water was being supplied, it would be a simple matter to haul the pipe up and poke in a few more holes. By flooding an area in this way, with the pipes only about an inch or two below ground, one uses far less water than if one tries to do it by over-flooding. There is so much less evaporation.

Perhaps one of the best plants for covering the ground in the shade of a tree is ivy. Some of our larger-leaved forms which grow luxuriantly are excellent for this purpose, and when the leaves from the tree above fall upon the ivy, it is only necessary to stir them around and allow them to fall beneath the ivy leaves, there to rot and form a beautiful mulch of leaf mould.

Start them young

IN gentler times, when there were far fewer distractions, it was easier to interest the children in the delights of gardening. Today, even if you possess a garden, it is not easy to inculcate a love of plants, and interest the children to a point where they are prepared to get their hands dirty and work at the rather dull jobs which are inseparable from gardening practice – the thinning, weeding, the hoeing, and so on. But there are now so many thousands of children living in towns who will never have the chance of sowing a seed, or picking a ripe strawberry.

On a recent visit to the New York Botanical Garden I was most impressed by the effort that is being made there to teach children the rudiments of gardening. In a fenced-in part of the Botanical Garden there is a large number of small plots in which the children work once a week under expert supervision to sow seeds and carry out all the normal techniques of cultivation. And greatly do they enjoy it.

In the suburbs of our big towns, where there is a certain amount of land available around the school buildings, school gardens are being established and they are very popular with the children. But in the big cities where the schools have no available land, the teaching of gardening is not easy. In a few towns the parks departments are providing plots where children can garden under the supervision of their school teachers, and one would like to think that there is active collaboration between the parks departments and the education departments to further this activity.

Having brought up two daughters from scratch, as it were, as far as gardening is concerned, I feel competent to offer one or two hesitant words of advice. In the early years the tiny tots wish to imitate mother and father and 'do some gardening'. This period is not very productive. About the age of six or seven the children demand a garden of their own. The temptation of course is to give them some out-of-the-way plot, but this is bad policy. What they really want is a plot that is bound to be seen and admired by all visitors to their home.

Give them a small plot to begin with, well prepared, with the promise of extension should they really make of job of it. Again, do not fob them off with any old bits and pieces that are not required elsewhere in the garden: let them pick out one or two of the best geraniums, pansies, or whatever you can spare, preferably either in full bloom or just coming into bloom, because children cannot bear to wait months for results. I make an exception here for tulips or daffodils, because they can plant these in the autumn and forget them for the winter. The bulbs of course are excellent because they can provide a wonderful show without much contribution on the part of the children.

What they like above all is something that they can call their own and can eat without having to ask permission. A small patch, say a few square feet, of 'Sparkler' radish, the red and white one, will mature in about twenty days from sowing, and a little row of spring onions, too, will be appreciated. One or two strawberry plants of their own, or maybe a gooseberry bush, will be highly regarded. Of course the little ones will eat the fruits before they are ripe, but they will learn in time.

A few years after this comes the pocket-money stage, the period when the children are keen to carry out some job of weeding a path, or raking up leaves to earn a few coppers. We tried this, but I think it is wrong because the work is tedious and boring, they tend to skimp it, and incur the wrath of the overseer, and in any case it does little to inculcate a real love of gardening. Far better to get them to come and help you weed a bed for a short time and try to get them to feel the same sense of satisfaction as the grown-ups do when a weedy bed is finally clean and presentable again.

One of my daughters decided to make a collection of flower stamps, and this we are doing systematically, devoting a page or more to each plant family, and writing the botanical and common names of the plants under the stamps. A good plant dictionary, once the child has been taught the way around it, gives the family, generic and specific names of most of the plants, although I must confess that some of the tropical ones take a good deal of tracking down. At least flower stamp collecting teaches the children that tulips and fritillaries are members of the *Liliaceae* and so on. It helps if the children are taking botany at school.

Every year unfortunately there are a number of fatalities through children eating the seeds or leaves of poisonous plants. Ideally, children should be taught never to pick and chew anything in the garden or from the hedgerows. They should be taught too that deadly nightshade, seeds of laburnum, and indeed many annual and biennial plants can be dangerous or even deadly. The daturas, normally only found on wasteland in this country in the form of *Daturus stramonium*, which has seed pods rather like a small green conker before the seeds come out of it – attractive to children because of this association – are deadly. The foliage of larkspur and foxglove, the leaves of tobacco plants, are all harmful, and the seeds of the castor oil plant, *Ricinus communis*, are deadly – even the leaves are harmful.

It is a good idea to warn children that all plants with a milky juice, such as milk weeds and spurges, are liable to cause trouble. Fortunately most of these plants have a very unpleasant bitter taste, and the children usually do not chew very much of them. But some children are unusual in this respect, and may persist.

It is always wise if a child shows symptoms of pain and drowsiness, headaches or vomiting to suspect that some harmful plant, or part of it, has been eaten. If by questioning this proves to be the case, it is wise to seize a specimen of the plant the child has eaten, and seek medical advice at once. If children, especially friends of your own children, are in the habit of visiting the garden frequently, it is wise to remove the seeds of any potentially dangerous plants, especially laburnums.

The June gap

WITH flowers, as with vegetables, there is often a period about this time of the year when there is little to cut in the garden. Naturally one can arrange to even out the supplies a little by the skilful use of cloches for both vegetables and flowers, but without this advantage the problem of having a few cut blooms at the end of May and in June is worth considering.

It is not always easy to remember when certain plants flower, and of course this varies from season to season and in different parts of the country. But it is worth while noting down in your diary the dates when the first flowers of any particular plant are ready for cutting, so that when the time comes to plant in the autumn a fairly reasonable sequence of cut flowers can be assured. This may sound a trifle obvious, but I know from my own experience that every year at some particular time we say we must make arrangements to have more cut flower material, and then we tend to forget about it when planting time comes.

We normally cut our first bunch of paeonies on the first day of June, and we pick pyrethrums earlier than this. These, together with some plants of the double *Thalictrum dipterocarpum* 'Hewitt's Double', and *Scabiosa caucasica* 'Clive Greaves', we grow across the end of the vegetable plot just for cutting. Among the paeonies some of my favourites are 'Felix Crousse' bright red, the very large silvery-lilac-pink 'Mme. Jules Elie', the white and salmon 'Solange', and the beautiful pink 'Sarah Bernhardt'. Of pyrethrums, 'Eileen May Robinson' and 'Brenda' are two popular cutting varieties, but there are many more available nowadays.

We find too, that by having a batch of Dutch irises in a cold greenhouse, and another lot outside, we can spread the cutting period of these useful flowers over several weeks, and they come at a time just before sweet williams, when the spring flowers, wallflowers, and the like are over, and there is not much to cut among the perennials. They are very cheap, and a good mixture contains quite a useful range of colours. On my light soil, and in a warm south-facing border at the foot of a wall, they increased vigorously for about ten years, and then for one reason or another began to dwindle away. While on the subject of bulbous irises, it is worth mentioning that if a moment can be spared, this is a good time to lift and dry off the bulbs of such small rock garden irises as *I. reticulata* and its varieties, and the yellow *I. danfordiae*. Some varieties of *I. reticulata* increase in certain soils, others do not, and if there has been a history of these irises dwindling away in your own garden, it would pay to go to the trouble of lifting them, drying them off gently now, and replanting them in the autumn. With *I. danfordiae* this treatment is almost obligatory in most gardens.

At the end of the first week of October we sow a row of sweet peas under cloches. To our delight we are able to cut our first bunch of sweet peas at the end of May, and in June they begin to flower well.

A dozen or so large plants of Regal pelargoniums in the greenhouse make a very useful contribution to our flower arrangements at this time. Many people, I find, do not realise that these flowers last quite a long time in water. They do tend to drop a few petals now and again, but for low dinner table arrangements they will last several days and with the range of colours now available are most useful. If one wishes to be rid of the labour of watering the Regal pelargoniums in the greenhouse during the summer, they may be planted out in the open garden now and will produce, with any luck, a large quantity of material to be used as cuttings if one wishes to increase the stock. Naturally they will have to be lifted, trimmed back, and repotted before frosts arrive in the autumn. Cuttings of the zonal types of pelargonium – the varieties we commonly know as geraniums – rooted now would make nice plants to give some flowers in the greenhouse during the winter.

Another plant that has proved extremely useful for cutting at the end of May and in the early days of June is that beautiful double, scented thornless rose 'Zephirine Drouhin', growing against a south-facing wall. Most of the shrub roses flower earlier than the modern hybrids, and are worth planting just for the purpose of securing some early cut flowers. Many of them, it is true, only flower once, but one cannot have everything.

Beating the weeds

IN 1967 a combination of slowly advancing years, increasing commitments, and the wettest May for nearly 200 years resulted in the most unmanageable crop of weeds we have ever had in the garden. This was in spite of every conceivable piece of equipment being to hand and the availability of chemical weedkillers and mulching materials. It was just not possible to find time when it was not raining to deal with the weeds.

Sowings had to be made, ground prepared for planting, urgent staking, spraying and other jobs had to be done, and the weeding and hoeing had to be left. Paraquat was useful on many areas; it can be applied in rainy weather perfectly effectively, as once it hits the leaves of the weeds, nothing will wash it off.

As everybody knows, even if you have time to hoe between the showers, you must collect up the weeds, otherwise they will root again. But not everybody realises that groundsel, grass weeds, and many others, can ripen their seeds even though they have been uprooted, if they are left on the ground.

But I did not set out to write about weed removal, rather about weed evasion or suppression. If, like my wife and me, you have come to the conclusion that hoeing and weeding take up too much time and cause too much fatigue and aching muscle, what are the alternatives? Broadly, they fall into four possible lines of action: intensified use of chemical weed control, more mulching, replacing more beds, borders or cultivated ground with grass, and much greater use of ground-covering, weed-smothering plants. I propose to dispose quickly of the first three alternatives.

Chemical weedkillers are not cheap when bought in small amateur's packs. Their use is limited, but where they can be used they are a godsend. The ordinary tar oil winter wash, for example, is excellent for controlling moss on paths, paving, and the like. Mulches are excellent: sawdust, mushroom manure, half-decayed leaves, bracken, straw, and so on, if available at a reasonable price, greatly reduce the work and give the bonus of keeping the soil more moist. They still have to be barrowed to the borders and spread among the plants.

More grass means more mowing, more weed-, moss- and worm-control, probably a new and larger mower, and bigger maintenance bills. So now my wife and I have decided that every square yard of our garden than can be furnished with ground-covering plants shall be so planted, even if it takes us two or three years. We will buy or beg from our friends every suitable kind of plant; we will propagate by cuttings, seed, or division every type of plant we already possess even if it means that for a year or two we have too much winter flowering heather or too many hostas. They can always be replaced by different plants as we come by them.

It is not really necessary to wait until October to start these plantings; 'canned' or potted plants may be bought at garden centres now and provided they are watered well in dry spells, may be planted any time. Also they will provide cuttings or pieces for division later in the year.

One of the most successful weed smotherers is *Stachys lanata* 'Silver Carpet'. This form produces no flower spikes, only a dense carpet of silvery foliage. The aubrietas, cut back early in the month, make new growths, and these are ideal to use as cuttings. The common purple kinds seem to spread faster than the double forms, so it is wise to propagate plenty of plants and pack them in fairly close together.

Heathers I will not dilate upon now, but merely put in the reminder that *Erica carnea* and its varieties grow on any soil and, given a little encouragement, bone-meal scratched in during the autumn, and water in dry weather, will cover large areas. A fairly

hard trim over now, if not already done, is necessary to keep them
bushy and tidy.

Many people, I know, have become a little tired of the old
bear's ears, *Bergenia cordifolia*. True, the old type plant, welcome as
the pink flowers are in April, is rather ordinary, but the newer
varieties are much more attractive. 'Evening Glow' with bronzy
foliage and reddish-purple flowers, and 'Silver Light', white
flowers with pink calyces, are a great improvement. The trick with
these plants is to place them next to later flowering plants, or to
plants with golden or silver foliage. The contrasts of foliage are
charming, winter and summer. Sun roses, varieties of helianthemum, are well worth planting, and the double forms are the best
to my mind, as the single flowered forms drop their petals at the
end of the day.

Visiting Beynac in the Dordogne, I came across a large stone
sink filled with a richly golden variegated form of ground elder.
I was just about to appropriate a small piece when I saw a beady-
eyed old crone watching me from a window. A friend, however,
spotted some in a restaurant near Moissac. He asked for a piece
and the patron said: 'Help yourself – elle pousse partout.' He is
now propagating it, but he thinks that, as with many variegated
plants, it is not so vigorous as the green form. Perhaps any ground
elder or, if you prefer, bishop weed, is a dangerous plant to
introduce to a garden, but I have many odd corners where it could
romp to its heart's content.

With this weed-control problem I have decided we cannot be
too horticulturally proud. The old snow-in-summer, *Cerastium
tomentosum*, given a corner to itself, is a wonderful weed smotherer.
Common it may be, but jolly useful.

For the autumn we have been propagating *Polygonum vaccinifolium*, which spreads quickly and smothers itself with pink flowers
in September. The leaves turn brown and remain on the plant
throughout the winter. It is a slow starter in the spring – indeed it
is only now beginning to push forth the new leaves.

Auriculas, easily raised from seed, or increased by division,
do not deteriorate in my light soil as do polyanthus. Indeed they

spread lustily, flower early in spring, and make a dense ground cover. They could be used more often.

It is perhaps necessary to make a distinction between evergreen, deciduous, and herbaceous ground-cover plants. Ideally one should look for those which have a massive coverage all the year round. The low-growing junipers are excellent and it is a bold weed that will try to penetrate their thick foliage. But ferns are useful. True, one may have to do some weeding around them early in the spring but from now on they will take care of weed growth.

One of the most useful ground coverers is *Sedum* 'Weihen-stephaner Gold', which came from the horticultural station at Weihenstephan near Munich. Incidentally, if one is touring Bavaria it is a fascinating place to visit, as the Director is patiently and exhaustively trying all the varieties of main garden plants to find the best and weed out the rubbish. He has already sorted out about 300 varieties of paeonies and chosen about three dozen of the best. The sedum, low growing and compact, is now covered with yellow flowers and in the autumn will delight us with bronzy foliage. It is easily and quickly propagated by division.

In most gardens there are hedges. Weeds grow beneath them. A watering with paraquat in the spring should keep them clean, but an underplanting of ivy, rose of sharon, *Hypericum calycinum*, or the non-flowering stachys would probably keep down weeds for the whole year. Naturally if one underplants a hedge with anything the hedge may suffer. So more regular watering and feeding with a good liquid fertiliser may be necessary.

I realise that some readers may say that I am adopting a defeatist attitude and that I am becoming an old gardening square. We still have five small greenhouses to look after. We still bed out our front garden in autumn and spring, and we still grow all our vegetables and a fair proportion of our fruit requirements. This evasive action of massive ground cover is only to enable us to go on growing these things, pot plants, and cut flowers for the house, without having a weedy garden that we must apologise for in April, May and June.

Jobs for June

BE more than usually alert for signs of attack by greenfly and blackfly - roses, strawberries, red and black currants and many other plants suffer from these pests. When walking round the garden, turn the leaves of plants over here and there. Very often these pests congregate on the underside of the leaves, and the first sign we see is a puckering or distortion of the leaf surface.

Black spot disease spreads quickly on roses, so once a week if you can spare the time spray roses and other plants likely to suffer from diseases and pests with a combined fungicide and pesticide. Hexyl Plus is a good combined spray for this purpose.

If you grow strawberries, put down straw or black plastic sheeting between the plants as soon as the fruit has set, not before. I prefer the black plastic sheeting because the slugs do not like crawling over it.

Raspberries are producing new shoots fast now, so remove all except those required to produce next year's crop. One strong shoot every 8 in. or so along the row will provide enough canes for replacement of this year's canes when they have carried their crop.

When the raspberry flowers are just about to open, dust them with derris powder and repeat the application ten days after the flowers have fully opened. If you miss this trick for any reason spray the flowers with liquid derris ten days after they are in full bloom, and repeat the dose ten days later. This will ensure maggot-free raspberries.

You should stop cutting asparagus about the twentieth of the month in the south half of England, and by the end of the month in the north. If June should be dry, give the beds plenty of water.

Sow the main crop of carrots, more lettuces, and another row of an early pea like Feltham First. As a gamble, sow another row of French beans for a late crop.

E   H.G.R.

Trim aubrietas hard back – give them a real army hair-cut. The young shoots that will very quickly appear make excellent cuttings if you want to increase your stock. Trim winter-flowering heathers fairly hard now but do not cut back into the old wood, only cut back last year's growth.

If you have a wisteria, nip out the young growths to leave only three or four leaves. This is important. Wisterias, like most apple trees, only flower on short spurs, never on a long bare branch.

There is still time to sow seeds of wallflowers, myosotis, cheiranthus, sweet williams, and other annuals, but get them in very soon.

July

One tends to think of September as the harvest month. So it is for the farmers, but if the gardener is not beginning to reap his harvest in July he has missed the boat. The roses are at their loveliest. The fruits and vegetables are coming in fast. The annual flowers and the perennials are at their best. In theory we should be sitting back a little now, pondering upon the garden's success or shortcomings; planning changes, new plantings, the elimination and replacement of mediocre plants. Too, we must remember that it is about this time that fruit trees and flowering shrubs make up their minds about what they are going to do next year. Next year's strawberry crop is being decided now. So more than at any time it is essential to keep up the level of soil moisture. Mulchings help enormously, especially as a mulch prevents the soil from becoming panned down in the torrential rains which we often have in the second half of the month.

But in general, July should be a lazy, reflective month for the gardener who has done his work well earlier in the season.

Trouble-free plants

A GARDENING journalist, naturally, is at the receiving end of every kind of cry for help because some particular plant has failed to perform satisfactorily or because diseases, pests, sickness or death from one cause or another have brought disappointment. In one part of the country it may be deer getting into the garden; apparently they have a tremendous fondness for roses. We sighed with relief some years ago when the rabbits disappeared, and now they are on their way back and once more people are asking for plants that rabbits will leave alone. Sometimes I find it necessary to leave my desk and take a walk round the garden just to reassure myself that we are not a nation of gardening masochists, and that there are many plants which survive and flourish with no trouble at all.

It may be defeatist to decide that plants that are always difficult, or always suffer from some pest or bird damage, should be eliminated. We are a nation of gardeners because we have responded to the challenge of the difficult plant, but it is depressing to go on year after year with plants that either do not like our garden or are the prey to pests, diseases, and other troubles. So for the gardener who wants a quiet life, or plenty of satisfaction without constant coddling and cossetting, it may be worthwhile to take a look at some of the plants that are, in the main, trouble-free.

Let us begin with some of the hardy flowers that rabbits do not like. (Incidentally, I have found that very few other pests take any notice of these plants which are usually rabbitproof.) High on my list is the red hot poker; all the different varieties of *Kniphofia*, and some of the dwarf orange ones, such as *nelsonii*, are really charming especially in a small garden; the good old nepeta, oriental poppies, eryngiums, the true hardy geraniums of all kinds, irises, rudbeckias, the lamb's ears – *Stachys lanata* – bergenia or bear's ears, which is valuable for its pink flowers very early in the year, and potentillas of all kinds, I have never known to be damaged.

Still thinking of herbaceous plants, I have in my own garden many which seem to be virtually immune from pest and disease attack. The delicately-cut leaved, yellow-flowered *Coreopsis verticillata*, *Lythrum* 'The Beacon', geums, aconites, the Japanese anemones, *Sedum spectabile* and its varieties, and the Greek Mallow, forms of sidalcea, phloxes, and many more consistently perform year after year without trouble.

Woolly aphis seems to be more widespread than it was some years ago. In the old days we used to have to brush the affected parts with a stiff brush and methylated spirit, but nowadays a B.H.C. spray will usually take care of this unsightly and very damaging pest. Maggots in the raspberries, of course, are always a perennial problem, but here again they need not be if we take the precaution of spraying them with derris when the first flowers open, and again about seven to ten days later.

But very often it is possible to buy one's way out of trouble if one is prepared to spend some money. For example, I have come to the conclusion that I am going to grow all my strawberries in future under cloches. I am increasing the stock of cloches so that as the first early crop is gathered, the cloches can be placed over the adjoining rows, not with the idea of hastening their ripening, but to protect them from slug damage, birds, rain, and the inevitable rotting that occurs if we run into wet weather at fruiting time. The same cloches can be brought into service again in the autumn to cover a row or two of the autumn fruiting varieties.

More and more I am turning to the shrubby plants, both tall and lowly, with attractive flowers or foliage, or in many cases both, because in the main they suffer from little in the ways of pest or disease. It is of course true that at this time of the year the shrub borders tend to be a trifle dull, but there are shrubs that will flower in late summer, caryopteris, *Spartium junceum* the Spanish broom, hydrangeas, and, of course, the beautiful golden hypericums such as 'Hidcote' which will make a bush 4 or 5 ft high, and the dwarf forms such as *H. moserianum* and the common old Rose of Sharon, which is such a wonderful plant for a dry bank. The Rose of Sharon, *Hypericum calycinum*, will put up with conditions that would defeat many other plants – the large beds at the entrance to London Airport are proof of that.

With a little careful planning we can easily arrange for colour in shrub borders throughout the summer and autumn. A few plants of the Japanese anemones would flower late in the year, lilies of course are a good standby, and if we are prepared to go to the trouble of sinking a few pots of, say, standard fuchsias, agapanthus, lantanas, and other greenhouse plants in among the shrubs to do their stint in the summer months, it is possible to keep the shrub border interesting from early spring until the frosts arrive.

Charming conifers

PERHAPS more than most plants the dwarf conifers arouse strong feelings of like or dislike among garden lovers. There are those gardeners who abhor any dwarf or stunted type of plant, and yet others who are so enthusiastic about the dwarf conifers that they become almost obsessed with them.

There is no doubt that in the modern idiom of gardening these plants are being increasingly used. Gardens are smaller, the tendency is to plant for permanence, and these conifers are exceedingly useful. Just as they exercise a fascination over certain humans, they also seem to be irresistible to dogs, and we have learnt by bitter experience in our own garden that it is a waste of time planting any dwarf conifer within easy reach of the path.

The only other difficulty we have encountered with dwarf conifers has been with that magnificent grass-green, shapely variety *Picea albertiana conica*, which was discovered in 1904 by Professor Jack and Alfred Rehder in the woods at Lake Laggan, Alberta, in the Canadian Rockies. This plant was growing happily on my rock garden until it became defoliated, presumably through an attack of red spider mite or aphis, to which it is rather prone. One must be on the watch with dwarf conifers to see that these pests are firmly kept under control.

The publication of a new handbook on the subject, *Dwarf Conifers*, by H. J. Welch (Faber, £4 4s), is an important landmark in the history of these plants. The author explains in considerable detail how these peculiar mutations, whether they be dwarfs or weeping forms, prostrate forms, colour mutations, and so on, arise in Nature, and why there has been so much confusion in the naming of these variants. He and others have spent many years collecting these forms, and collaborating with specialists at home and abroad to clear up confusion in their nomenclature. His book will be welcomed no less eagerly by horticultural writers, who have hesitated to write more often about dwarf conifers because of the confusion in the nomenclature, than by those who like to have their plants correctly labelled.

The conifers described in the book, the author assures us, are all available in the trade, although some may require seeking out from the nurseries that specialise in these plants. It must be emphasised that the plants described are natural dwarfs and not those that are artificially kept dwarf by root pruning and a semi-starvation diet such as is exercised by the devotees of the Japanese art of Bonzai. These Bonzai trees, too, are becoming extremely popular, and imported plants are now available at quite reasonable prices. These plants are normally slow growing, and one has to be patient with them. The impatient among us can always obtain a quick effect by planting a few of the more rapid-growing conifers and removing them after, say, ten years or so, by which time the true dwarfs will have made a fair amount of growth, and will be showing up to advantage.

My own favourites among them are the golden forms, or those that have golden tips to the foliage. Among the latter, *Thuja* 'Lutea Nana' is a great favourite of mine, and I am delighted to see that Mr Welch considers it should be made more use of in gardens. It is interesting that the golden-yellow colour is much more maturely developed in winter, when it is most to be desired. We have it with the feathery *Chamaecyparis pisifera* 'Filifera Aurea', where we can see them every day throughout the winter from our dining-room table, and when a shaft of sunshine touches them in winter the effect is really enchanting.

But without necessarily developing a collector's passion for dwarf conifers one should make more use of them in gardens large and small. The tremendous variation in habit can be used to great advantage. The many prostrate conifers, forms of juniper, for example, are wonderful weed-smothering plants, and with the years will spread and eliminate hours of recurrent hoeing. Then there are the 'bird's nest' conifers such as *Chamaecyparis lawsoniana* 'Nidiformis', and C. L. 'Tamariscifolia', or the many spreading varieties of *Picea abies*, all of which are desirable plants.

Naturally these dwarf conifers are in demand for rock gardens, but there are many other places where they can be used to advantage, and indeed they never look better than when given a position of prominence associated perhaps with one or two beautifully weathered rocks set in an area of close mown turf.

Mr Welch's handbook, the result of many years of painstaking work, will undoubtedly become a standard work of reference on the subject. But it is more than that. Throughout the book there is the distillation of many years of practical experience, and the author's enthusiasm is reflected in practically every description.

Gardening in towns

WHEN my garden was open to the public one year, more people asked the name of the grey foliage plant *Leucophyta brownii* than anything else in the garden. It is an unusual plant, a mass of thin, silvery stems, and it can either be tied up to a short cane, or, as we use it, allowed to hang down over the edge of a tub. It is, unfortunately, not hardy.

We could, I feel, make much more use of silvery-foliaged plants than we do, especially to relieve the solid colours of summer bedding schemes. In this respect I am reminded of the days before the war, when my father bedded out in the royal parks all kinds of silver-leaved plants, including one or two scarce types with woolly leaves. Within a day or two, the sparrows had stripped them bare to line their nests, to my father's fury. I have even known them to do this to some plants of the old lambs' ears, *Stachys lanata*, in my Surrey garden.

Whether certain races of birds develop mischievous habits periodically or not, I do not know, but I have observed that our sparrow population in recent years has taken to all kinds of devilry, which it never performed before. They tweak off the buds of my wisteria; they peck at certain plants in the rock garden, particularly the yellow spring-flowering *Alyssum saxatile* and in a friend's garden they deliberately removed all the stems off a dozen thymes she had planted, and left them lying on the ground.

In the country we have our troubles, but town gardeners have even more, and those who try to garden among the bricks and mortar would find *Town Gardening*, by Leslie Johns (Collins Nutshell Book, 5s) not only a mine of information but very entertaining to read. Leslie Johns is in the happy position of having a very beautiful roof garden in the centre of London – in Covent Garden in fact – and another garden he is making in the country. Most gardening books are written textbook fashion, and only now and then do we come across a book that really reflects the character and enthusiasm of the author. This book does. He says, for example, that he believes strongly that the gardener should be the boss, and not the garden. With this I entirely agree, whether we are gardening in town or country. There are plenty of plants which will grow in any garden if only we take the trouble to seek them out, and by so doing we shall save ourselves many heartbreaks.

The author lists the plants – climbers, carpeting plants, rock-garden plants, and so on – which will survive town conditions. He deals with virtually every aspect of gardening in towns, and I endorse strongly his penchant for water in a garden no matter how small. Today with submersible pumps, precast imitation stone fountains, fibre glass pools, and so on, it is really simple to install some form of moving water.

In his selection of trees and shrubs he endorses what has long been known about town gardens, that the best plants are those that lose their leaves in winter, or spend the winter underground like herbaceous plants or bulbs, but he does include a number of evergreens, the strawberry tree, *Arbutus unedo*, for example, the Japanese laurel, *Aucuba japonica*, camellias, which surprisingly are happy in town gardens, *Euonymus*, *Fatsia japonica*, the sweet bay, *Laurus nobilis*, and surprisingly, *Olearia haastii* and *Osmanthus delavayi*.

When it comes to rock-garden plants, the town gardener is in trouble. I remember years ago a wealthy man purchased outright one of the rock gardens at Chelsea Flower Show, and had it removed to his garden in Hampstead. After twelve months all he had left was a heap of rocks and a large quantity of labels. But the real stalwarts of the rock-garden world – *Alyssum saxatile*, arabis, oxalis, London Pride (*Saxifraga umbrosa*), houseleeks, and aubrietas will survive. So will bergenias, the winter-flowering heathers, and the old Rose of Sharon, *Hypericum calycinum*.

Here I enter a proviso: if one is prepared to go to endless trouble creating the right soil conditions, protecting alpine plants from the winter by propping sheets of glass over them, there are many more plants that can be grown. Before the war a gentian lover in Golders Green managed to grow an enormous range of gentian species and varieties. In fact, his garden consisted of little else.

Reverting to trees and shrubs, it surprises me that Mr Johns does not make greater play of the genus *Magnolia*. He only mentions *M. stellata*, but I have seen wonderful trees of *M. soulangiana* and others growing in front gardens in the main streets of Hamburg, and even in front of a church on 5th Avenue in New York. The laburnums, flowering cherries, almonds, and even peach trees grow well in towns. In Holloway Road there used to be, years ago, a wonderful peach tree that carried heavy crops of fruit every year, to the great temptation of the local children.

Some years ago we made a number of recorded broadcasts for the B.B.C. in Bavaria and one of these included an account of what the Munich city council described as their 'allotment gardens'. These were quite delightful, covering about 30 acres in one corner of a new park. The idea was to provide a leisure activity for the flat-dwellers in which the whole family could participate. Several different types of chalet could be purchased, erected on site, with water and electricity laid on, and the family could spend the week-end there or odd days. They were obviously very happy. The gardens were a delight. If for any reason the owner of one of these family gardens had to relinquish it, a valuation was made, taking account of the improvements carried out over the years, and Munich city council bought it back.

Now the idea is catching on here. Cardiff has a similar scheme under way, Birmingham is about to embark on one and recently two of these 'new style' family gardens were shown to the public for the first time at the headquarters of the National Allotments and Gardens Society at Flitwick, Bedfordshire. Mr Fred Willey, M.P., who visited these gardens was full of enthusiasm and I hope many local authorities will study these pilot schemes and find the resources to set up similar projects.

There is, I am sure, a trend towards the growing of fruits and vegetables at home again. If the town dweller can have a plot where he is encouraged not only to grow some fresh produce, but also to beautify it with shrubs and flowers, it will give him and his family endless pleasure. The C.I.D. sergeant whom I interviewed in Munich, and his family, were devoted to their family garden and spent most of their leisure hours there. Of course, as one would expect, on this site there was an attractive building with a bar where the residents meet in the evenings, drink beer, and even have light meals and either discuss their horticultural problems or have a good old sing-song. Anyone interested can get further information from Mr W. France, The National Allotments and Gardens Society, 22 High Street, Flitwick, Bedfordshire.

Of this and that

AT a recent show of the National Sweet Pea Society there was a tremendous number of amateur entries, but there was only one trade group, and I am afraid that this must be regarded as a sign of the times, since sweet pea growers are finding it too expensive to show regularly.

By the same token, top quality sweet peas fetch quite high prices in Covent Garden Market, even as late as early July. Sweet peas and indeed the culinary variety are well worth while growing at home, and if one keeps the sweet peas assiduously picked so that no seed pods are allowed to form, they will go on producing blooms for many weeks. At Chelsea Flower Show there are usually fine exhibits of salpiglossis – those beautiful, upturned trumpet-shaped flowers in many colours, mostly veined and laced, and irresistibly recalling a stained-glass window in a church. They can be grown from seed sown in the spring and planted out when danger of frost is past, but grown in this fashion they never reach more than about two feet in height. If, however, the seeds are sown at this time of the year, the seedlings potted off and kept in a cool greenhouse throughout the winter, they make much bigger plants which may be put out in the garden at the end of May.

Curiously enough, this plant objects bitterly to fog. In fact a really good dense London fog will finish off a batch of salpiglossis even in a greenhouse. But my father, when he was in charge of the Central Royal Parks, used to grow large quantities of these lovely plants, and found that simply by covering them with newspaper at the first sign of a fog, they were completely safe.

Turning to more mundane matters, this is the time when we must be even more pest-conscious than usual. It would pay now to take a walk round the garden and examine hedges and large shrubs to see whether there is any infestation of aphis. Normally we are too preoccupied watching our precious roses and other plants to suspect hedges and large shrubs of being a source of infestation. If one is on good enough terms with the neighbours, it might be worth while examining their hedges and shrubs, as they too could be providing a take-off point for pests, and with a little co-operation a spray programme could be jointly undertaken and save a good deal of trouble.

Some plants seem to have a peculiar attraction for slugs – the hostas, or funkias as they used to be called, *Phacelia campanularia*, that bluest of blue annuals, even strawberries just as they are becoming ripe. But now we are hopeful that the new slug killers made by Adco and I.C.I., with a greater concentration of metaldehyde, will give us a far better control than we used to have with the old slug pellets.

Every year one determines to do better but only too often the weather or pressure of work defeats us. In my own garden we have plenty of room at the end for dumping lawn mowings, weeds and other garden rubbish. As a result, we tend to make several heaps, and just leave them for a year or two to rot down, and then we spread the 'compost' on the garden and dig it in, or use it as a mulch. But over the years we have come to the conclusion that this lazy way of making compost is not all that clever, because the weed seeds in the compost survive and grow to plague us when we put it on the ground.

If we had less space, we would use one of the compost 'converters', which would rot down the raw material fast, generate a lot of heat in the heap, and with luck destroy the weed seeds. Short cuts in gardening we have, plenty of them, but sometimes it pays to take a little more trouble. Of the converters in popular use, Adco, Bio and Garotta are all very efficient, and in a matter of weeks in summer will rot down the garden waste.

The summer cauliflower is a crop that pays really handsomely for watering. It detests any kind of a check, and regular watering especially at the time when curds are forming is most rewarding. My wife always complains about the caterpillars that infest these cauliflowers. She soaks them in hot water and this dislodges the caterpillar from the heart of the curd. The caterpillars are those of the cabbage white butterfly. The main infestation which migrates here from Scandinavia usually arrives in late summer, so it is wise to spray these summer cauliflowers with a suitable insecticide as part of the regular spray programme.

I think we often underestimate or fail to recognise the damage done by strong winds. I once saw a number of flowering cherry trees on which the leaves were half curled inwards. Being short-sighted I just thought they had been attacked by aphis earlier on, but this was not so. As the worst affected trees were in the most exposed position it was obvious that strong gales were the cause.

Gales not only cause leaves to transpire moisture at a great rate; they cause bruising which prevents the leaves from functioning properly. Indeed it is probably the force of the gales rather than the salt they carry that causes damage to trees and shrubs in coastal districts. Dr R. H. Stoughton once proved by experiments in a wind tunnel that the browning of foliage similar to that caused by coastal gales could be produced simply by high velocity wind with no salt content.

Variety in the greenhouse

A YOUNG Tahitian woman visiting our garden one day was highly amused to see us growing *Lantana camara* in the greenhouse. 'But it's a weed', she said. 'It grows all over Tahiti.' It is, however, an excellent plant, very free with its orange flower heads, and it grows quickly in a greenhouse with a minimum night temperature of 45° F.

Indeed, it is surprising how many lovely plants can be grown in what to many people is an absurdly low night temperature, and if soil warming is installed they can be persuaded to flower that much earlier. With a small, electrically heated propagating case, raising seeds, or rooting cuttings is easily done, and it is surprising how quickly and cheaply stocks of various plants can be built up.

Not only are flowering or foliage pot plants very useful to bring into the home in winter when cut flowers are scarce and dear, but they are handy for grouping in a *jardiniere* or other container at any time. In these days when help in the home is minimal, there are times when the housewife is relieved to have pot plants to save her the trouble of arranging cut flowers.

Among plants that can be raised from seed now are cinerarias and calceolarias. Some people do not like the fat 'pouches' of the calceolarias, but the Multiflora strains are neat and compact, and there is a good range of colours nowadays. Again, with cinerarias, most people prefer Multiflora mixture, or separate colours, because they fit into small rooms or combine well with other plants in a *pot-et-fleurs* arrangement.

The gaily coloured coleus, I have discovered, do not like the B.H.C. vapour that our Aerovaps constantly diffuse to control pests. Since we have grown them in a house where we do not use B.H.C., they have excelled. It is quite remarkable how modern strains of coleus have been improved since the days I inspected contract crops of them being grown for seed in the south of France. From a small packet of seed there will be perhaps two or three dozen plants with hardly two identical.

The modern streptocarpus strains are large-flowered and come in a mixture of lavender, blue, pink, rose, red and white. Particularly good forms are easily increased by leaf-cuttings rooted in a propagating case. They will tolerate a temporary stay in a living room, but because their large leaves transpire moisture fairly fast they need regular and generous watering.

African violets, varieties of saintpaulia, I admit do not take kindly to my greenhouse conditions. They need a higher temperature than I can afford – 55° F. at least. I have a feeling that they too do not like B.H.C. If you have a small section of a greenhouse that can be kept economically at 55° F. they should be quite happy. Again, they can be raised from seed in a propagating case at about 70° F.

The butterfly flower, schizanthus, if sown in August will

produce neat flowering plants in spring. They need plenty of light because they tend to become drawn and spindly in low light conditions, or if they are packed too closely together; give them plenty of room, if necessary scrap some of the plants to give the others a better chance.

A gardening journalist should be catholic in his tastes, but he would be less than human if he did not have his particular favourites. Some plants I find less fascinating than others, and in this category I include the cacti. Now, before anybody leaps to write and say that I am being biased or unkind to cacti, may I record that the flowering cacti and other succulents, mammillarias, echeverias, zygocactus, epiphyllums, and so on are very attractive. They are on the whole easy to grow. Also, from a packet of seed one can raise quite a fascinating collection of genera and species. Furthermore they grow surprisingly quickly. It is even possible to grow the so-called 'pebble', or 'living stones' succulent plants, forms of mesembryanthemum, from seed. These look like pebbles and if planted among stones in a trough or plastic tray, never fail to interest the young or old.

Some people find *Primula malacoides* difficult to grow. Certainly it may be affected by botrytis in dull humid weather in autumn and needs plenty of ventilation. Much easier is *Primula obconica*, which will put up with considerable neglect as regards watering, and does not mind widely fluctuating temperatures when brought into a living room. These and the yellow-flowered *P. kewensis* may all be sown now for flowering next year. One must make the point that some people can contract a rash from *P. obconica*.

The strelitzias, or Bird of Paradise flower, are perfectly happy in a cool greenhouse, either in pots or planted in a border. They grow by the thousand in cold glass structures in North Italy, and from there the gorgeous flowers are exported all over Europe. They last a couple of weeks in water, and therefore command quite a high price in florists' shops.

Of the foliage plants, the forms of *Begonia rex* and the green *B. masoniana* with its almost black 'iron cross' marking, are also quite content with these low night temperatures. Yet I find they flourish in a centrally heated home. One must, of course, take care with these and other begonias in a greenhouse, not to allow water to touch the leaves; hot sun will cause browning if it strikes leaves with water on them.

Jobs for July

TREAT lawns with selective weedkiller if necessary; moss often appears in many lawns in July, but a mercuric moss-killer will prevent it spreading. The lawn should have a good dressing of fertiliser about ten days before applying selective weedkillers, but do not put the first two or three mowings after applying the weedkiller on the compost heap – burn them. Mow lawns more lightly at this time of year and in hot weather allow the cuttings to lie on the lawn.

Continue to spray against pests, mildews, rust, black spot, and other diseases. Remove dead flowers from rhododendrons and azaleas.

Prune out any dead branches from flowering shrubs.

Root cuttings of aubrietas, arabis, genistas, cytisus, and similar plants.

Line out seedlings of wallflowers, myosotis, and other biennials intended for bedding out in the autumn. Keep them well watered in dry weather.

Stake and tie gladioli, dahlias, and chrysanthemums. Disbud dahlias and chrysanthemums if large flowers are required.

Feed tomatoes and cucumbers regularly, using a fertiliser specially compounded for these plants.

Plant out leeks and winter greens. Lift and dry shallots.

Summer prune fruit trees, red and white currants and gooseberries.

When the strawberry crop has been gathered, trim off all the old leaves and spray with an insecticide against aphis. Order more plants if required; if planted in August, they will crop next year.

While the greenhouse and frames are relatively empty, they should be scrubbed down with water containing a household disinfectant. Any repairs or necessary painting may be done now.

Treat wooden fences, gates, pergola posts, and the like with a wood preservative such as Cuprinol, *not* creosote. Metal gates and metal frames should be given a rust-proof undercoat before painting.

August

Looking back over the years August is a month that is either hot and dry or depressingly stormy and often wet. Either way this poses problems for the gardener. If it is wet the weeds grow apace and on our return from holidays the garden is a depressing sight. If it is hot and dry the crops hasten towards their close, the lawn turns brown, and we have to be prepared for the curtain to fall on our year's labours. But if we have been wise enough to plant deliberately for late summer and autumn colour we shall see a pleasing dividend. If not, we can take note of the gaps, look around in other gardens and at shows, and determine to remedy the defects for another year.

Now, too, one can start again, building steps, or walks, repairing fences and doing the work of maintenance or reclamation that was left in abeyance earlier on.

Home from the holidays

THE moment when it is time to leave one's holiday haunt and head for home is always sad. But once on the way there is the anticipation of one's own bed, home cooking – and the garden. How will it have fared?

In my own case, three weeks spent on the rocky but delightful shores of Corsica made a tremendous difference to the garden at home. The prunus hedges that we planted to act as a screen to our new neighbours made at least 18 in. growth in that time. In their third year they are now nearly 10 ft high.

The multiflora sweet peas, which we grew for the first time, are over 8 ft high and still flowering prodigiously. They have been in bloom and giving us five, six and seven blooms on a stem since the end of July. Because we begged the staff and neighbours to keep them well picked they look like flowering for several weeks yet.

The gladioli have romped away in our absence and are in full bloom. This year there seem to be none of those peculiar brown-leaved oddities that often appear as the result of diseased corms, and which should be removed and burnt lest they be harvested later along with the healthy corms.

Modern research has shown that there is no point in leaving gladioli in the ground once the flowers have faded. They may be lifted and dried for storing during the winter and planted again next spring.

The sweet corn is late but still promising.

I made a small bet with myself how long it would be before my wife broached the subject of a greenhouse just to grow those wonderful climbing plants that so delight us in Corsica and along the Côte d'Azur. She raised the subject in that superb oblique way which I know so well, by asking if the pink bignonia that festooned the arbour on the terrace of our friend's house in Corsica was hardy in Britain.

Poker-faced, I had to admit that it was not so hardy as the rich orange bignonia which one sees all over the west of France, and which will grow outside quite happily in the southern half of Britain. She then referred to our friend's borders flanking the drive to his house in Corsica, which he has planted entirely with pale flowers – blues, pinks, and white, with grey or silver foliage.

Here he has the pale blue plumbago with pink geraniums climbing the walls, white agaves, pink and white oleanders and the like. He takes the view that in a hot climate there should be no hot colours in the garden – no scarlet zinnias or cannas, nothing but the pastel shades. He is entirely right, and the effect is charming. Even in our tepid British climate I would think there are parts of the garden where these pastel shades could be usefully employed. After all, it is the light colours that show up so well in the evening light, and many of us see our gardens only in the evening and at the weekends.

The discussion about these half-hardy plants was resumed after dinner, and it soon became apparent that my wife is determined to have a greenhouse devoted entirely to those plants that need such protection against frost as can only be provided by a house kept just above freezing in the winter. Secretly I have always wished for just such a house and I am glad to say that my wife is already planning economies to liberate the £15 or so that will be required to pay for the electricity to keep the house frost-free in the winter. There are so many lovely plants that one can grow in such a cool greenhouse. Yellow and white jasmine to flower in February, bougainvilleas, hoyas, streptosolen, passion flowers, and many more can be grown up the wall and over the roof of a cool greenhouse. In the ground or on benches there are dozens of plants that just need frost-free conditions in the winter to flower for weeks or months.

Returning from holiday we realised that we had not ordered our hyacinth, tulip, and daffodil bulbs for growing in pots and bowls for the winter, but there is no hurry. Dr van Slogteren, who for many years was in charge of the bulb research station at Lisse in Holland, used to complain bitterly that bulb merchants and journalists in Britain urged people to plant their bulbs far too early. His experiments have shown that planting in the first or second week in October gave the best results with the exception of tulips. So we are still in time, but in order to obtain the varieties one desires there should be no time lost now in placing the orders. Any good bulb merchant can supply pre-cooled daffodils and tulips which will flower at Christmas or shortly afterwards, and hyacinth bulbs which have been so treated to flower thus early.

Tough roses

IN the Royal National Rose Society's publication *Roses, A Selected List of Varieties*, which is only obtainable by members of the society, there is a selection entitled Beginners' Roses. These are hybrid tea varieties which are recommended because of their hardiness and vigour for unfavourable positions, towns, industrial areas, and other places where it might be thought that rose growing was a bit of a gamble.

It is interesting to note that the list includes 'Super Star', 'Prima Ballerina', 'Gail Borden', 'Wendy Cussons', 'Grand'mère Jenny', that beautiful new yellow rose 'Grandpa Dickson', 'Fragrant Cloud', 'Ena Harkness', and 'Peace'. What interested me is that in this selection the white 'Frau Karl Druschki' and the pink 'Mme Caroline Testout', both sixty-seven years old, 'Lady Sylvia', born in 1927, 'Betty Uprichard', from the 1921 vintage, and 'Ophelia', which was the first rose whose name I learnt at my father's knee during the First World War, are classified as first-class roses for beginners in unfavourable situations.

Bulbs for Christmas

MOST of us, in spite of all good resolutions, tend to chase our tails as far as gardening tasks are concerned. We put off thoughts of the winter and the spring while the days are warm and sunny, but a gardener must think at least six months ahead, if not more. So we should now be turning our thoughts towards bulbs for growing in pots or bowls to give us blooms for Christmas and early in the New Year.

Every year I receive many complaints that bulbs have failed to perform well, so perhaps it would be worth while to run over the basic principles of success with bulbs indoors. The type of container is most important. Eschew all bowls with shallow sloping sides. Choose those that have if possible vertical sides and which are at least 4 in. deep. A bowl of this depth is sufficient to accommodate one layer of bulbs, but if you can find a container say 7 in. or 8 in. deep, it is then possible to grow two layers of bulbs, one on top of the other, and this makes a truly superb effect when they are all in bloom. We use old copper coal buckets, jam pans and the like, but in recent years we have tended to use 8 in. clay pots with a double layer of daffodils or tulips, and then bring these into the home and bed them in peat in the copper jam pan. In this way we can keep the jam pan furnished with two or even three successive batches of bulbs. It may be objected that these copper containers are now difficult to find, and very costly, but soon to come on the market are fibreglass replicas, moulded from the originals, with a copperised finish which is indistinguishable from the real thing and which, to the joy of the womenfolk, never needs to be cleaned. These are much less expensive than the real article.

I am often asked about the growing medium for bulbs in bowls and other containers. If the bowl has no drainage hole, then obviously one has to go for prepared bulb fibre which is only peat with the addition of charcoal and some oyster shell grit. But if there is a drainage hole, as for example in a flower pot, then I use the ordinary John Innes or Levington potting compost, and I feel the results are usually slightly better. I am sure that if you wish to grow the bulbs in the garden after they have done their stint in the home those that have been grown in a good compost will be in better shape to re-establish themselves in the garden than those that have expended their energy in a compost that has virtually no nutritional value.

Bulb fibre suffers from the trouble that it is very difficult to wet once it has dried out. The bulb fibre should be thoroughly wetted before use; the old guide is to squeeze a handful and if a little water just oozes out between the fingers, it is at the right moisture content. If a bowl should dry out then it must be stood in a bucket of water for a little while to soak, then tipped on its side to allow any surplus water which has accumulated at the bottom to drain away, and thereafter watered assiduously.

Many people believe that it is essential to put bowls or pots of bulbs in the dark while they are making their roots. Darkness is not essential. What is important is the temperature. The bulbs need to have a period of anything between eight to twelve weeks in the coolest spot that can be found for them, to encourage root action. Ideally they should be placed outside in a shaded, north-facing spot, and covered with a 4 in. or 5 in. layer of peat, leaves, straw, or some other covering. I prefer peat to the other materials because slugs do not seem to relish burrowing down through peat to get at the young, succulent shoots. The only time we had real trouble with bulbs was when we covered them with straw. If it is not possible to place the bulbs outside, then the coolest spot in the house should be chosen, whether it is dark or not.

One of the commonest failures with bulbs can be traced to impatience on the part of the grower – the bulbs have been brought into the warmth before they have made adequate root growth. Normally a daffodil can be brought into the living room when there is about 2 in. of growth above the soil in the pot or bowl.

With tulips, again, 2 in. is usually sufficient, but with practice one can feel with finger and thumb the tiny swelling of the embryo bud in the shoot above ground. So long as the embryo bud is clear of the bulb, then the tulips will grow in balance. If they are brought in too soon they will make vast quantities of leaves and the flowers will be almost hidden in the foliage. With hyacinths you should wait until the bud is well clear of the bulb; then they can be brought indoors and they will make a perfectly balanced plant. Timing is all-important.

Nowadays we can buy quite an impressive range of bulbs that can be persuaded to flower at Christmas, and even more that will flower early in the New Year. There are a dozen varieties of hyacinth, specially prepared for Christmas flowering, that may be planted in the first week of October, and at the same time we could plant pre-cooled daffodils in such varieties as 'Golden Harvest', 'Patria', 'Texas' the charming double variety, and several more.

Tulips need to be planted rather earlier, about the middle of September. They can be brought inside about December 1, and grown on in a warm room should flower by Christmas. A remarkable new variety 'Christmas Marvel', a rosy-carmine flower, lasted for nearly a month in our home from Christmas onwards last year.

Sometimes I fear bulbs which have rooted well out in the open suffer when they are brought indoors. They must grow accustomed to warmth and light gradually. Put them in the coolest room – in the hall perhaps – for a few days, and if there is too much light, cover them with a sheet of newspaper for the first two or three days. Then when the foliage has greened up, accustom them gradually to warmer temperatures. After a week or ten days they will be capable of supporting the normal room temperature of 65–70° F. But remember that no plants like fuggy, smoky atmospheres. Keep them growing in rooms that are not liable to become befugged with tobacco smoke, and only bring them into the really public rooms when they are in full bloom.

One excellent way of growing bulbs in bowls or pots is to bury them in the ground in a north-facing border so that the top of the pot or bowl is at least 6 in. below the soil. If the bowls are precious, they can be wrapped in newspaper to prevent any scratching of the glaze. Naturally you have to mark the spot where they have been buried carefully with some stakes, then after about ten weeks it is possible to take away the soil and examine the bulbs. If they are at the right stage for bringing in they can be lifted immediately, if not they should be covered up again and left for another week or two.

The small bulbs – crocuses, snowdrops, muscari and the rest – in my experience do not like to be grown for long periods indoors. It is better to leave them outside until they are on the point of flowering, and then bring them in. In this way one can have them two or three weeks earlier than in the open garden.

With a little care and attention to these details it is well possible to succeed every time with bulbs grown in pots or bowls to flower indoors in the depths of winter.

Before the war we used to import millions of crowns of lily-of-the-valley from Germany for forcing at Christmas time. These were grown in Pomerania and lifted in the spring when they were dormant. They were packed in boxes and placed in cold stores in Hamburg and sent out from August onwards.

As a result of this treatment, the crowns hurried into flower and indeed would produce blooms within three to four weeks of planting in pots or bowls. In those days in the large private gardens, the gardener was always expected to have plenty of lily-of-the-valley in bloom for Christmas. There is now an adequate supply of crowns for forcing, and if these are planted in moist peat in early December and kept at about 50° to 55° F. in a dark place until the leaves are three or four inches high, they will flower easily for Christmas. As soon as the foliage has made about three or four inches of growth, the bowls or pots should be moved into full light, and of course, kept adequately watered.

Naturally there are plenty of varieties of hyacinths, daffodils, and tulips that can be planted in pots or bowls to flower from January onwards, but to be sure of flowers for Christmas, order in August as supplies are rather limited.

Ornamental hedges

I AM often asked about training roses and other plants as hedges and ornamental screens. Naturally, a great deal depends upon the soil and situation, and the purpose for which the screen is required. If something fairly quick growing is wanted, then the delightful poplar, *Populus candicans* 'Aurora' is an obvious choice. If a screen of only about 10 or 12 ft in height is required, or even lower, it is possible to buy these poplars as quite small trees, around about 4 ft, and then keep them pollarded, that is to say trimmed over, when they have reached the desired height.

This way one gets a bushy head on the tree, and is able to enjoy the extraordinary foliage at quite close quarters. This foliage opens with a pinkish tinge; in summer it turns to a pale creamy colour flaked with green, which if planted against a dark background is especially pleasing.

One of the problems about screens of living plants is that too often one cannot afford sufficient space to allow lateral growth without having the trouble of trimming them. Let us first consider hedges that may be close-trimmed. The beech or hornbeam are of course excellent, and all withstand close trimming. So will the various types of prunus hedge. These prunus hedges are grown on their own roots, and are very vigorous. I have one of the green myrobolan interplanted with the purple *Prunus pissardii*, which is now about 10 ft high after six or seven years. Others, four years old, have made very good growth; we trimmed them back to about 5½ ft this year, but they could easily reach 6 or 8 ft in another twelve months. These prunus hedges – there are several varieties on the market such as 'Sloepink' and 'Trail Blazer' – will make rapid growth provided they are given plenty of nitrogen in the spring – they are gluttons for nitrogen – and adequate water. We give our hedges about an ounce and a half to two ounces of sulphate of ammonia to the yard run, scratched into the soil in the spring. Those that have grown best are in positions where they can receive plenty of irrigation. One hedge has been much more slow growing because we have not yet got around to equipping it with its own irrigation system.

I would suggest that anyone contemplating planting a hedge should begin to clear the ground now, working in plenty of manure or compost so that the site has settled well before the hedge plants arrive in the autumn. It would also be worth while to arrange for adequate watering by laying a length of Alkathene pipe to the plot and attaching to this a length of punctured Alkathene or one of the ready-made punctured plastic spray lines. When there are many other plants in need of water in the garden, I feel we tend to forget the hedge plants, and if we want rapid growth, water during the dry weather in the formative years is essential. With these prunus hedges, do not be in a hurry. Cut them down to about six inches or a foot above ground and they will make about three or four feet in the first year, and this should be cut back to about 2½ ft the following spring. Carry on like this until the hedge is the required height.

If there is plenty of lateral room in the garden for the hedge or screen, it is not necessary to trim these hedges so severely. To get height, of course, one has to be fairly brutal, but need not trim side branches quite so severely unless one wants a really close, thick hedge that does not take up too much space.

With *Cupressocyparis leylandii*, again given some judicious feeding with bone meal or some similar fertiliser, and plenty of water when required, rapid growth can be obtained, and one does not have to keep shortening the plants as one does with the prunus hedges. Let the plants grow to 4, 5 or 6 ft, and then begin to trim them.

Most people want evergreen hedges for privacy, but deciduous screens do act as a filter for traffic noise. An excellent screen can be made with *Pyracantha rogersiana*. It may be clipped hard if necessary, but if it is not clipped too much it gives lavish flowering, and then its autumn berries. I would not plant it in very cold exposed places, and it does need a certain amount of support when it is young. It is an excellent screen for an ugly fence or garage. *Cotoneaster henryana* makes an excellent short screen where there is plenty of room, and trimming is not necessary.

Even if the green fronds of the bamboos can become a little tarnished in bad winters, they still act as a perfectly good screen, and are well worth planting. They have been a little scarce in recent years, but I gather that stocks are now building up and they do increase fairly fast. The Sea Buckthorn, *Hippophae rhamnoides*, with its silver leaves and twigs, makes an excellent screen, and is particularly useful in exposed coastal districts. If one provides support, such as the square-meshed, plastic-covered wire panels, or some kind of trellis, the evergreen honeysuckle, *Lonicera henryi*, is excellent. I also grow the golden variety *L. japonica aureo-reticulata*, but I find it does not seem to romp away as well as *L. henryi*.

Late border flowers

BEHIND our old farm house we have two borders of hardy flowers that we see from our dining-room window. From time to time we think of scrapping them as they do need quite a lot of attention, but we cannot think of any other way of filling these two borders so that we get some colour for most of the year.

The trouble, of course, is that we expect too much from them. We like to start with the golden doronicums, *D.* 'Spring Beauty' or the taller *D.* 'Miss Mason' in April, with purple honesty. Agreed we cheat a good deal in these borders, leaving space for biennials, tulips and annual flowers to follow.

Then, since we like the garden to be at its best when visitors come round in June and July, we continue the display with a few bearded irises, erigerons, oriental poppies, hemerocallis, paeonies, campanulas and other summer flowers. The kniphofias or red hot pokers, whether they be red, orange or golden, carry on the display, but at the end of August there is a hiatus. The michaelmas daisies are not yet out, the phloxes are just beginning to look a little worn and sometimes the aconites finish early.

We intend to plant *Aconitum wilsonii* 'Kelmscott Variety' in the hope that it will give us its bright blue flowers really late in the season. The grey-leaved *Anaphalis nubigena* with fairly large white heads of papery 'everlasting' flowers on 2 ft stems is one of the bright spots and of course we should have near it some clumps of *Sedum spectabile* 'Autumn Joy' with its pink, bronze-tinged flat heads of flowers.

The obedient plant, *Physostegia speciosa* 'Rose Bouquet' is just coming into its own and we are hoping it will not become too invasive, as in my light soil these plants, like some michaelmas daisies, do tend to wander and become a nuisance.

I would dearly like to grow the *Alstroemeria ligtu* hybrids in their lovely shades of pink but I do not at the moment have a place for them. Quick-draining soil they must have and this we could provide, but they do best in a warm border at the foot of a south-facing wall and the only ones we have are full of lilies, hemerocallis and *Nerine bowdenii* which I do not wish to disturb.

If anyone wishes to try these alstroemerias, and they make wonderful cut flowers, I would suggest ordering pot-grown plants for spring delivery or growing them from seed in spring. Sow one or two seeds in a seed-sowing compost in peat pots: I find the square variety of peat pots excellent because they nest nicely against each other when standing in a seed tray and do not dry out so fast. Thin the seedlings down to one in each pot and grow them on for planting when large enough. They resent disturbance, so plant them peat pot and all. Even in a sheltered border such as I describe it is wise to put a covering of 6 to 8 in. of straw over the plants in winter to protect them from severe frosts.

There are, of course, dozens of plants that one could grow for late summer and autumn but in a limited area there must be a compromise.

How I used to envy those fortunate folk like the late Sir Philip

F   H.G.R.

Sassoon, who had superb herbaceous borders at Trent Park planted just for a June display, and others at Lympne for August; or the people who had the June–July gardens in the south and the Scottish gardens from August 12 onwards. How much easier for their gardeners too.

Jobs for August

THIS is a good time to take cuttings of many plants. Pinks, brooms, hydrangeas, pelargoniums, Japanese azaleas, camellias, indeed most shrubs, can be propagated by cuttings now. But in hot weather make sure that the cutting frame is kept very well shaded and moist.

If you are growing a few plants of the 'winter cherry', *Solanum capsicastrum*, spray the flowers when they appear with one of the so-called 'hormone' tomato setting sprays. All good garden stores sell them. One spraying of the flowers as they open will ensure a good set of the orange fruits.

Keep chrysanthemums, dahlias, and gladioli well supported. If you want large flowers on your chrysanthemums, and dahlias, disbud them now. Watch for any sign of disease on these plants and mark any that show mottling of the leaves for destruction later on. Spray chrysanthemums and dahlias once a week against pests. Ring the changes – say B.H.C. one week, and derris the next.

Spray roses and michaelmas daisies once a week with a fungicide to keep mildew and black spot under control.

Prune shrubs that have flowered in the past few weeks. Philadelphus you keep productive by cutting out some of the old stems to make room for the new ones. With weigelas, cut the stems that carried flowers back to where a strong new shoot is growing. Trim back genistas and cytisus by cutting away about one third of the stem that has been produced this year. Do not cut into old wood.

Try to complete all hedge trimming in August. Hedges trimmed later may produce young shoots that will be soft and vulnerable to frost damage in winter. Trim lavender and rosemary now.

Keep French and runner beans, also marrows, assiduously picked. Never leave any pods or marrows to grow too large, otherwise the plants will stop producing any more.

If you want to plant a new row of strawberries and pick a reasonable crop next year, get them planted in August or early September.

If you are growing tomatoes outdoors, and four flower trusses have formed, nip out the growing part of the plant. We can seldom ripen more than four trusses in the open in Britain.

If you have young children and you are growing a few marrows, scratch their names on one young marrow with a nail file or a ball-point. As the marrow grows large so will the names. It is guaranteed to amuse and it costs nothing.

September

The season draws to its close. The last bursts of colour with the dahlias and the last of the brightly coloured annuals take it out gloriously. But even now we are thinking about the spring. Bulbs to grow indoors should be ordered now. Trees, shrubs, roses and hardy plants that we wish to plant between now and March should be ordered before stocks run low and we may have to accept substitutes.

The days close in, but a golden autumn, with misty mornings and cloudless days, can be the most precious time of the year.

No need yet to cut down and clear out the remnants of the summer flowers. Still to come are the delights of autumn colour. But it is time to think of building a greenhouse if this is in the programme for next year. Set up and equipped in the next few months, it will be ready for business, for forcing the bulbs we shall be planting soon and raising the seeds we shall be sowing after the turn of the year. September is usually a kindly month.

Preparation for planting

EVERY worth-while hobby presents a challenge; that is its fascination. In stamp collecting, running a string of racehorses, or even playing poker, the length of one's purse is usually significant. So, too, in gardening, but to a lesser extent. There is no doubt that a long purse can sometimes hasten the desired results in a garden. It is possible to find large specimens of rhododendrons or azaleas that can be moved with success, but these are naturally fairly scarce and expensive.

Before the war, when labour was fairly cheap and plentiful, nurserymen used to grow plants on for a number of years, moving them from one part of the nursery to another to encourage the formation of a fibrous root system. They could then be sold to the customer at five to ten years old and capable of re-establishing themselves in their new lodgings.

In those days we used to be able to buy yew trees, 6 ft high, which would transplant with no danger of loss; but since the war the nurserymen have not had the labour to spare for this annual transplanting, the demand for trees and shrubs has been so great that they have been able to sell all their plants the moment they were large enough, and now the supply of large plants is limited in the extreme.

In some ways this is a good thing because small hedge plants, trees and shrubs, young and vigorous, transplant well. If they are well fed and watered they get away to a flying start, and very often make far better specimens in a few years than much older plants would have done. I would, however, emphasise the necessity of preparing planting sites well for all trees and shrubs. Except on very wet soils, the incorporation of generous quantities of peat in the planting sites pays handsome dividends.

When a tree or shrub is to be planted, a hole should be made to the depth of a spade, the subsoil well broken up then slightly firmed again. The excavated soil should be mixed with peat – up to 50 per cent is not too much – and when the tree is planted its roots should be covered with this peat and soil mixture. I have found over the years that the addition of bone meal – a double handful to a bucketful of peat – helps enormously to get the shrubs, trees or roses away to a good start.

It is possible to move quite big trees with success and achieve an air of maturity to a landscape site very quickly. Trees from 12 ft to 18 ft high are now being moved, but only if they have been properly prepared in the nursery. For successful transplantation these trees need a compact and fibrous root system. Periodic root pruning and transplanting is necessary to achieve this, and generous quantities of peat worked into the ground at each transplanting encourage a mass of fibrous roots capable of supporting a large head to the tree.

Indeed, with these techniques it has been found possible to transplant trees up to 40 ft high. The line of trees planted in Kingsway recently is an excellent example of the value of the new technique. Incidentally, when trees of this age are planted they are usually old enough to withstand any attacks by vandals. Experimental work on this problem and upon the feeding of rhododendrons, azaleas, and other shrubs has been carried out by Fisons Horticulture Ltd in collaboration with Mr Edmund de Rothschild in his garden at Exbury.

It goes without saying that the larger the tree or shrub the more care must be given to it during its first year or two. A heavy mulch or layer of peat, straw, bracken, half-decayed leaves, or other material should be put on the ground around the plants, and care should be taken to see they do not suffer from lack of moisture.

Three years ago I acquired a plot of land adjoining my garden; I kept a half-acre strip to protect my flank and sold the remainder to a builder. We planted a long line of *Prunus pissardii nigra*, the purple plum, which makes such a magnificent hedge up to 6 ft high in a matter of three years. On the same day the neighbour planted a similar hedge from the same batch of plants. My hedge was watered and fed conscientiously and is now at least three times as high and as thick as the neighbour's, which was left to take its chance.

As part of the tidying-up process, we planted a large semi-circular bed of shrubs, at the foot of a sixteenth-century barn which I acquired with the site. All the rainwater from the roof of this barn falls upon the semicircular bed. It contains a number of climbing roses, to screen the wall, *Genista lydia*, a large purple buddleia, *Senecio laxifolius*, hydrangeas, and such plants as aubrietas and *Polygonum vaccinifolium*, so beautiful at this time of the year with its bright pink spikes of flowers and reddening foliage hanging over the low retaining wall of the bed.

Immediately opposite this bed the neighbour has planted a collection of shrubs, but so far has not been able to lay on water to them. The difference between the growth in the two beds is staggering, and is an object lesson in the value of water on a light, quick-draining soil. But even in this age of impatient hustle, it usually pays to be patient and plant young vigorous trees and shrubs.

This is an excellent time of year to prepare the ground for an asparagus bed. Planting can be done in March or April. Thorough cleaning of the ground, the removal of all perennial weeds, deep digging, and the incorporation of plenty of manure or compost are essential to get the plants away to a good start. With modern methods of weed control asparagus is really no trouble, and I am surprised that more people who have ground to spare do not grow this delectable vegetable.

Flowers for arrangements

IT is with diffidence that I write about plants that may be grown especially for flower arrangements. I have seen beautiful gardens almost ruined because the lady of the house has become a fanatical flower arranger and has planted all kinds of shrubs and herbaceous plants, annuals, ornamental grasses and the like simply to provide her with precious 'material' and with no regard for the effect these plants will make in the garden. Of course it may be argued that apart from observing a few local by-laws, the garden and what use we make of it is one of the few fields of human activity where we still have complete freedom of action. If one wishes to make it into a sanctuary for golden pheasants and homing budgerigars, or a production line of flower-arrangement material, it is entirely at the discretion of the garden owner.

So I offer a few suggestions of plants that may be grown with flower arrangements in mind. The devoted flower arranger will of course know most of them; she will already have on her bookshelf *The Ilford Book of Flower Decoration* by Joan Groves (Ebury Press, 15s), which illustrates and describes many unusual plants, and *Shrub Gardening for Flower Arrangement* by Sybil Emberton (Faber, 30s). The suggestions which follow are for people who wish to have plenty of flowers and foliage for cutting but who are not necessarily trying to win prizes at flower arrangement exhibitions.

For the owner of a greenhouse, even a small one, the many varieties of *Begonia rex*, *B. masoniana*, the variegated ivies, such as *Hedera* 'Chicago' and others, and even a grape vine will provide much useful foliage for use in flower arrangements. The range of flowering plants is almost infinite.

In the open, too, many variegated ivies may be grown, and there is a host of plants that may be used to fill odd corners and provide useful foliage – the hostas, in various shades of green, variegated yellow or white, are excellent, provided one is prepared to protect them, if necessary, against slugs, by putting down slug bait regularly. The variegated hollies are useful and so are the mahonias, the variegated forms of elaeagnus, the grey-leaved *Senecio laxifolius*, the Japanese maples in green or fiery red, and for autmn arrangement the russety foliage of azaleas.

A plant that should be grown more often is that huge-leaved vine *Vitis coignetiae*, which turns to a vivid red in autumn. Ideally it needs a pergola, but an old and worthless apple tree would provide good support for it.

The flower arrangers make great use of shrubs, both for their flowers and for their foliage – the Smoke Bush, *Rhus cotinus foliis purpureis*, is one used for foliage, but I find the young foliage does not last well in water. But large-leaved trees and shrubs are popular; magnolias, and if the soil is acid, rhododendrons, yield much valuable foliage.

The flower arranger is always looking for the unusual in flowers or foliage. The good old standbys that we can grow in an odd 'cutting garden' – the gladioli, dahlias, chrysanthemums, pyrethrums, blue or white scabious – are obvious choices. But there are many hardy flowers that are not only decorative in the garden but intriguing when used as cut flowers. They also have the advantage of being virtually trouble-free – free, that is, from pests or diseases. The single and double forms of *Gypsophila paniculata*, although along with asparagus fern it seems to be a trifle *demodé* nowadays, is still a good garden plant. So are the alstroemerias, and if the lovely pink 'Ligtu Hybrids' are a trifle tender and a little difficult to establish they are still well worth taking the trouble to make them happy. They need quick-draining soil and a sheltered spot. The orange *Alstroemeria aurantiaca* I have found less difficult to establish. The bleeding hearts, varieties of *Dicentra*, are delightful in flower arrangements and will grow happily in semi-shade. The white spikes of *Cimicifuga racemosa* can often be seen in prizewinning exhibits at flower arrangement shows; it is another plant that is no trouble. So too are heleniums; and aconites which are so valuable at this time of year when blue, apart from michaelmas daisies, is rather scarce in the garden.

Red hot pokers of all shades of colour, bergamots (varieties of monarda), liatris, paeonies of course, and, if a damp spot is available, the globe flowers, varieties of trollius, are all excellent cut flowers.

If there is room in the garden for plenty of hardy flowers these, carefully chosen, should provide cutting material from April until November. Alan Bloom's excellent book *Perennials for Trouble-free Gardening* (Faber, 7s 6d) is a mine of information.

Window boxes

THANKS to the 'Britain in Bloom' campaign, thousands of tubs and window boxes have been planted in British towns and have added not only to the pleasure that overseas visitors have found in Britain but to the day-to-day life of us who live in these islands.

Strangely enough, there is very little literature about window boxes. This gap has been filled by Xenia Field, who has written a book entitled *Window Box Gardening* (Pan Books, 5s).

It is a very competent little book. It describes the various types of window boxes and how to make a wooden box. It gives advice on the kind of soil to fill it with, how to buy plants, what kinds to buy, and how to grow them.

Window boxes, if properly managed, can provide at least three productive seasons. They can be planted in the autumn with bulbs – daffodils, tulips or hyacinths – which will flower from the end of March to the end of April. They can then be planted with begonias, geraniums, petunias, pansies, and many other flowers which will carry on the display until the end of the summer. Then the summer flowers can be removed and the boxes filled with dwarf chrysanthemums, the small pompon flowered types such as 'Denise', to carry on the display until the frosts come.

Ideally, one should have two sets of window boxes, one to be filled with early-flowering daffodils, and the other with, say, dwarf tulips. As the daffodils fade they could be removed and replaced by the tulips. In a similar manner one could go on through the summer always having a window box in reserve to replace a box that is looking a little tired.

Nowadays we have window boxes made of expanded polystyrene, very light, very cheap, and from my own experience very long lasting. I have a window box that has carried two crops of flowers each year for the past six years, and it is still perfectly sound. Then we have window boxes made of glass fibre, moulded from original lead boxes and finished to look so much like the lead original that it is almost impossible to distinguish between the imitation and the prototype.

Window-box gardening is easy. Today one can buy from any good garden shop a bag of compost in which all the plants one would like to grow in a window box will grow quite happily. One can also buy a bottle of liquid fertiliser which will provide the added nutrients the plants need, and this can be watered in about every ten days.

Bear in mind that window boxes must be firmly anchored to the window-sill. It is possible for a freak storm to whirl an untethered window box off its sill and injure an innocent passer-by.

It is possible to plant permanent evergreens in a window box and to put flowering plants between them for display in the summer months. In the winter time the evergreens give a certain amount of pleasure. One can plant small box bushes, or dwarf conifers, which will last for years if they are well looked after, even in the confined space of a window box. In towns their leaves will be covered with a sooty deposit, and they will have to be washed forcibly with a syringe every two or three weeks to keep them clean.

In a small town garden or a courtyard it is possible to grow many plants in tubs. Roses, even climbing roses, can be grown thus, and clematis, hydrangeas, camellias, rhododendrons and many other plants will happily exist for years in the confined space of a tub. Good soil at the beginning and generous feeding afterwards is the right way to go about it.

Where the garden is behind the town house the soil may well be sterile and worn out, needing replacement every two or three years. Then plants have to be purchased at a high price, and the maintenance of such a garden can be a costly business. But if one is prepared to spend a certain amount of money on tubs, window boxes, and other containers, which in themselves are ornamental, a very charming effect can be achieved with little annual expenditure.

Two or three bags of soil for the containers, and very few plants, will create a charming effect. With glass fibre and plastic plant containers, today's town dweller can easily and reasonably cheaply have a charming garden, and these modern containers have their place even in country gardens.

We may live in an ersatz age, we may detest plastic flowers, frozen vegetables and the like, but we can at least accept plastic plant containers and use them to great advantage.

Chrysanthemums

WHEN some years ago it was discovered that by juggling with the day length it was possible to have chrysanthemums in bloom all through the year, many of us gloomily forecast that people would become tired of the chrysanthemum and that all-the-year-round blooms would not be popular.

We should have had more sense. It is possible to have perpetual flowering carnations at the florists on any day in the year, and the chrysanthemum lasts far longer as a cut flower than the carnation; indeed, cut chrysanthemums are a wonderful buy because, with careful management, removing the lower leaves and changing the water frequently, they will last for two or three weeks in a cool room.

The advent of the dwarf, pot-grown chrysanthemums was another milestone in chrysanthemum history. These neat little pot plants, which again are on sale all through the year, last for several weeks and are most useful for putting into window boxes in the summer, for use in *jardiniéres*, or in what is now known as *pot-et-fleurs* arrangements in copper jam pans and the like.

At this time of the year many gardeners are just about to bring their pot-grown chrysanthemums into the greenhouse where they will flower from November onwards. Nowadays there are some very excellent chemicals to use for spraying the plants before they are brought into the house to protect them against mildew and pests. It is always wise to spray the plants before housing them and, of course, the house should be thoroughly cleaned and disinfected, either by spraying or by the use of an insecticidal smoke cartridge before the plants are brought in.

But chrysanthemums suffer from virus disease which cannot be cured. Such chrysanthemums have malformed flowers with quilled florets, and are useless. It is possible now to buy rooted cuttings of chrysanthemum plants free from this disease. For the past three or four years I have ruthlessly thrown out all my chrysanthemum plants after they have finished flowering. I then buy rooted cuttings of virus-free plants, which are delivered about the end of August.

We plant these in the greenhouse about 18 in. apart each way, and these provide flowers from about the middle of December until the middle of January. We choose a selection of varieties that will provide a succession of blooms over this very important period. We grow one or two spray varieties and two or three varieties to produce large flowers, and on these we take just one bloom to each plant. We fix a length of square meshed plastic-covered wire at knee height, which is all the support the plants require.

As with many plants, the development of the chrysanthemum has been a slow but relentless process. If one could cast one's memory back even twenty years, one would be amazed at the development of the early-flowering chrysanthemum which can be grown outdoors. Now it is possible to produce blooms 8 in. or 9 in. across, four or five blooms to a plant in the open air. To obtain really fine blooms it is necessary to protect them from the weather, but it is easy enough to erect some kind of plastic shelter over the plants.

In the past ten years great strides have been made in breeding varieties of the early-flowering chrysanthemums, the incurved blooms, or the rather looser decorative types, and there is a wonderful range of colours today.

I would suggest to anyone who grows chrysanthemums either for the greenhouse or for planting in the open to obtain early blooms, that he makes a clean start next year and buys in virus-free rooted cuttings. If he can afford it he will scrap the old plants and start again each year with new stock, but it is possible to keep the old roots on and take cuttings from them for a year or two, and then discard the stock and start again.

Very few people know about the 'Charm' chrysanthemums. These can be raised from seed in a greenhouse in February; the young plants are pricked off into small pots and then moved into $4\frac{1}{2}$ in. pots in due course. The plants may be kept outside throughout the summer, and brought into the greenhouse by the end of September.

In October and November they make lovely domes of colour; the flowers are small, single, but are produced in great abundance. The plants can be brought into the house to give pleasure for many weeks. When these 'Charm' chrysanthemums are grown from seed, there is a good deal of variation; some are more compact than others and some colours are rather wishy-washy. So one selects a few plants for propagation by cuttings for the next year.

The chrysanthemum has come a long way, but the breeders have concentrated on producing new varieties for cutting, and have not put the same effort into producing new varieties for planting in our garden borders. It is true that we have many fine pompon and spray varieties that make excellent garden plants. It is also true that there are chrysanthemums that are hardy enough to be left in the ground throughout the winter – varieties of *Chrysanthemum rubellum*. The Korean varieties will also survive all but the severest of winters.

It is to be hoped that the breeders will work upon the problem of producing really first-class chrysanthemums to grow in our borders, and it is not too much to hope that one day we shall have chrysanthemums with large flowers in a wide range of colours that will be hardy in British gardens.

Choosing climbers

ONE winter a wooden pergola where we were growing half a dozen clematis collapsed, and I decided not to replace it. A neighbouring birch tree had grown much bigger in the fourteen years since the clematis were planted, with the result, aided I am afraid by some neglect in pruning, that all the clematis flowered mainly on the top of the pergola out of sight. So we dug them up, cut them back to about 4 ft above ground, and planted them elsewhere.

In my innocence I thought it would be easy to buy a few of those 'sprogged' poles, young saplings on which the side branches are cut back to about one foot. These form a very useful support for climbers and it is easy to do any necessary tying. I tried nine different firms without success. Finally, as a favour, one firm had some specially cut for me.

I hope I shall not offend too many architects if I say that some of the houses I have seen on my travels would look a good deal better if they were camouflaged with attractive wall climbers. Anyone having a home built might have the builder fix vine eyes between the bricks at suitable intervals as the house is being built.

It is quite a labour driving these into hard concrete; it is necessary to make holes with an electric drill. Once the vine eyes are in position, of course, it is easy to fix either plastic-covered wires or the plastic-covered square meshed wire panels to them.

It is always refreshing to read Brigadier Phillips's work because he packs in a great deal of simple information not often found in gardening books, and his *Climbing Plants for Walls and Gardens*, (Heinemann, 25s) is no exception. I fully share his ecstatic enthusiasm for wisteria. I do not prune ours as methodically or as severely as he recommends. His method is to pinch all new shoots back in summer to leave five leaves. In winter he prunes these shoots to leave only two buds. We usually nip the shoots back in summer to leave anything between two and four leaves and we get plenty of growth and flower buds.

Whether we get any flowers depends upon how efficiently we protect the buds against sparrows. This we do with black Scaraweb, but it has to be teased out, or more has to be put on if it becomes too matted with snow or rain. One tends to think that birds will leave the buds alone when they are an inch or more long. Not our sparrows; they suddenly decide to spend a day tweaking off the buds, as far as I can see simply to pass the time.

Brigadier Phillips says, so rightly, that wisteria does not mind having its roots in full sun. But like many such plants, I am sure you will get better growth if a large part of the root area is paved over. In our small cottage garden at Grayswood we had two wisterias, one against the house wall, the other on a garden fence. Both were planted together. The one on the house had its roots under concrete paving and was truly enormous, reaching to the eaves and around three sides of the cottage. The other covered only about 10 ft wide. Soil is always moist under paving.

Most of us, I suppose, are not sufficiently adventurous about the choice of wall plant. We tend to go for climbing roses, jasmine, wisteria, or even virginia creeper: all excellent plants, of course. Some of the most desirable and beautiful of climbers are hardy enough to grow only in the milder counties, and even these may be killed or cut severely back in a really bitter winter. One has to weigh the risks and decide if one is philosophical enough to take them.

Personally, if I have had say ten years of pleasure from *Fremontia californica* or *F. mexicana* with their masses of yellow saucers, the waxy pink bells of *Lapageria rosea* or its white variety, the lovely white passion flower *Passiflora* 'Constance Elliott', I feel I have had my money's worth. Our passion flower has been cut to the ground three times in the past five years, but has survived; in 1967 it was laden with flowers and carried a heavy crop of fruits.

A word of warning about the lapageria. It prefers to be planted on the north side of a wall and then hang over to flower on the south side.

The climbing potato, *Solanum crispum*, will reach to the top even of a three-storeyed house. Then the actinidias, *A. chinensis* and *A. kolomitka*, always excite curiosity when they are well established with their large leaves produced in generous quantities. The plant produces creamy flowers and small fruits like a gooseberry – edible, but to my taste not very exciting.

But one could go on almost indefinitely. Anyone who has a considerable area of wall or fence, who is prepared to erect pergolas, poles, or other supports for climbers or wall shrubs, or who has a greenhouse where so many lovely but tender climbers such as the blue *Plumbago capensis* may be grown, would find Brigadier Phillips's book not only an inspiration but loaded with hints and all kinds of interesting incidental intelligence about these exceedingly useful plants.

Leaves of autumn

GENERALISATIONS about gardening can quickly run into deep water. Take this simple example. A reader wrote to ask about leaves. Was it desirable to gather up all the leaves all over the garden in the autumn, or could they be left until the spring? Is it wise to put a mulch – a thick layer of leaves – on beds and borders in the autumn, or should this be done in the spring? Is it right that rose leaves and apple leaves should be gathered up and burnt because of the danger of carrying disease over to next season?

Let us consider the simplest problems first. Certainly rose and apple leaves can carry over disease and I much prefer to put them on the bonfire. Theoretically, all leaves may be put on a compost heap and if it is properly managed so that adequate heat is generated, disease spores and pests are supposed to be destroyed. But in the late part of the year and in winter it is not so easy to generate this amount of heat in the heap, so I burn all suspect leaves. If you have plenty of room, of course, you can make an

enormous heap of all the garden debris, cover it with a thick layer
of soil and leave it to rot for two or three years. By that time it
should turn into very useful and harmless composting material.
Even so, I would burn diseased material.

I am often asked if one may put such leaves as laurel, holly and
the like on a compost heap. As far as I know, there is no type of
leaf that should not be placed on a compost heap. The only
proviso is that hard shiny leaves take much longer to rot down than
the soft leaves of chestnut or lime, for instance, so it would be
preferable to put the tough leaves on a separate heap.

Now we have the problem of whether to let the fallen leaves lie
on beds, borders and among fruit trees and bushes for the winter,
or to gather them up now. There are really three considerations
here – aesthetic, hygienic and physical. Naturally the garden
looks much more satisfying if one can clear it all up before
Christmas. Indeed my father, who was trained in Scottish gardens
in the last decade of the past century, had an absolute mania for
having all swept up and dug over before the end of the year. In
Scotland bad weather and snow were almost certain after Christmas, so it was imperative to get the work done early. To the end
of his days he strove to have the clearing up done at least by the
New Year; then he could sit back through January and February
if the garden was covered with snow, and not worry.

There is much to be said for taking the hygienic point of view.
Leaves carry disease; they shelter slugs and snails and other
vermin. I would advise all gardeners, especially those who have to
garden on clay, to dig in the leaves and other debris in the autumn.
All clay gardens should be dug over in the autumn, if possible,
and left rough so that the frosts can break down the surface soil,
allowing it to be raked down fine for sowing or planting in the
spring.

Now we come to the question of the advisability of spreading a
mulch, or layer of leaves or peat, over the ground in autumn,
among any crops whether they be fruits or borders of herbaceous
plants or shrubs. Such a mulch will undoubtedly keep the soil
warm in the winter. It would protect the roots of tender plants from

severe frosts. But if left in place too long in the spring it would prevent the sun's rays from warming the soil in March and April. So it would have to be dug in fairly smartly in the early days of March.

To sum up, one could gain by having a mulch of leaves on the soil until early March, but not on clay soils.

Turning now to the mulching in spring: if you have accumulated a large heap of leaves, or if you are prepared to buy peat, old mushroom dung or sawdust, much toil and trouble can be saved if these materials are spread two or three inches thick over the beds and borders and among the fruits and vegetables. They conserve moisture in the soil. They suppress weed growth and render hoeing unnecessary. Although a few weeds will push up through the mulch and a few wind-borne seeds may germinate on the surface of the mulch, these are easily dealt with. But if you have a sufficient quantity of mulching material, do not spread it over the ground until about the end of April. It acts like an insulating blanket and prevents the sun from warming up the ground in these crucial weeks in spring.

Leaves can be a problem, but if they are available in quantity and are properly stacked to rot or partially rot they can also be tremendously useful. So it would pay to acquire a large quantity of leaves now. The local council's leaf-gathering squad will usually be only too happy to drop off a load of leaves at your front entrance. It saves them driving them back to their dump.

Plea for an early frost

IT may sound ridiculous to suggest that, as far as gardeners are concerned, the onset of some frosts earlier than they normally arrive would be a good thing. When autumn is soft and mild, growth on shrubs is soft too. Thus when we have the first really severe frost in November many plants suffer, both in gardens and in nurseries. Plants need a little 'hardening off' in the autumn

just as annuals or geraniums do when we move them out from
the greenhouse into frames and thence to the garden in the spring.
Some years ago we did not have these mild frosts. When the first
one came it was very severe, and all my honeysuckles were killed
to the ground. They have grown again, but it will take a year or
two before they cover their allotted space.

Again, an early frost or two will put paid to the display of
summer flowers in beds and borders. There will be no temptation
to leave them for another week or two and thus delay the planting
of the wallflowers, cheiranthus and other spring bedding plants.
These should be planted in October, whether the summer flowers
are finished or not. Planted early they will have the chance while
the soil is still warm to make new roots that will help them to
survive periods of drying cold east winds in the winter.

Bulbs for the greenhouse

BULBS and corms, both indoor and outdoor, are Nature's gift to
gardeners, and of course to children who, after the first essay into
horticulture with mustard and cress on a piece of flannel, usually
graduate to growing a few bulbs. Nothing in gardening is
infallible, but the 'prepacked' nature of a bulb, with all the plant's
parts in embryo contained inside, offers every chance of success,
provided we supply the simple cultural requirements.

There is much joy to be obtained if you possess a cold greenhouse
and are prepared to invest in some of the small bulbs which really
need to be grown at breast height so that their beauty can be fully
appreciated. Indeed a small cold house in which to grow alpine
plants and alpine bulbs offers a fascinating hobby, especially for
those who because of age or infirmity are unable to stoop. All the
work of potting, repotting, and tending the plants can be done at
breast height, or even sitting down.

So many true alpines dislike the winter damp of Britain: at

home they would be snug under their blanket of snow. But in a well ventilated cold house they can usually be grown perfectly. Naturally they need shading in summer, or they may be placed outside.

Among the bulbs the miniature cyclamen are some of the most attractive. At least a dozen varieties are obtainable today; some, such as *C. cilicicum*, *C. europaeum* or *C. neapolitanum*, with rose or pink flowers, and *C.n. album*, the white variety, flower in the autumn. For the spring *C. atkinsii* and its various forms, *C. coum*, again in several varieties, and *C. repandum*, a rich rose-pink variety with marbled leaves, are all exquisite.

Miniature narcissi, of which there are dozens of species and forms, are best admired at close quarters, and the small bulbous irises which flower early in the year are safe from snow and storm in a cold house. Not that these bulbs must have winter protection – they will grow well in the open – but under cover the risk of damage is removed.

The snakes-head lilies, forms of fritillaria, often with their delightful chequer-board markings, gain immeasurably when seen at close quarters, although they can be very effective once they establish themselves in quantity in the open. This they will do by seeding themselves if the soil suits them. On my light, quick-draining soil they do not spread. But a friend on the almost blue Reigate clay has them by the hundred in grass under light shade; it is some compensation for having to work his intractable soil.

At a recent show of the Royal Horticultural Society the members of the newly formed Nerine Society staged a lovely exhibit of these glorious greenhouse bulbs. In recent years many new colours have been bred, pinks, red, wine-coloured, and the size of the flower heads is being increased all the time. It is a pity that they are not hardy and need frost protection. Perhaps now that the genus has achieved 'specialist society rank' we may yet see other hardy forms arrive to join the deep rose *N. bowdenii* which is so welcome in the borders at the present time. Planted at the foot of a warm south-facing wall it increases generously, or did for me until by an oversight in the autumn of 1962 I omitted to cover the bulbs with peat before the bad winter set in. We lost many bulbs, and are now laboriously building our stock up again. We have found it hardier and more willing to increase than that other lovely autumn-flowering bulb *Amaryllis belladonna*, but both are so welcome just now in the garden or as a long-lasting cut flower that I do not grudge any small attention in the way of winter protection that they may need.

About autumn crocuses – the species and varieties of colchicum – we have mixed feelings. Naturally, we appreciate their goblets of pink, mauve, lilac, or white flowers in September or October, but to enjoy this autumn treat we have to put up with the rather large and unexciting foliage in the spring. Still, if you have a corner under a tall tree, or at the end of a shrub border which can be seen from the house, and which perhaps would not be made much use of otherwise, a planting of colchicums might be a rich investment. There are double forms too, but while I have nothing against doubleness in flowers generally I have never felt that the colchicum gained anything by thus greatly increasing its number of petals, or as we should correctly term them, perianth segments.

The colchicums are planted in August or September, and bloom in a few weeks. I remember how fascinated the visitors to Hyde Park used to be when they suddenly found, on one of their daily constitutionals past the dell at the eastern end of the Serpentine, hundreds of these autumn crocuses. They have this endearing habit of appearing quite suddenly.

Returning to the greenhouse, heated this time, we could with profit make more use of the hippeastrums. These huge and gorgeous flowers, known before the botanists insisted on a change of name as amaryllis, are equable, long-lived and undemanding plants. They like to remain undisturbed in their pots for years, provided always they are fed with liquid fertiliser during their growing season. They can be accommodated for several months in the winter, while they are dormant, under the greenhouse bench. Then in the early part of the year they produce their flowers and can be brought into the house for a week or two at a time when flowers are scarce and dear in the shops.

A versatile compost

EXCEPT for the fortunate few who have access to rich pasture,
and who have the labour to stack loam to rot down, then to
sterilise it and mix it into seed-sowing or potting composts, the
loamless composts have become essential. I suppose it is possible
to buy good well-rotted loam, but the ordinary amateur finds it
exceedingly difficult. Thus we welcome the new loamless compost, which has been developed after years of painstaking research
at the Levington Research Station of Fisons Horticulture Ltd. It
has been developed after many grades of peat were tested in
different millings, and consists entirely of peat with added
fertilisers.

It has many advantages for the amateur, and indeed for the
professional. It needs no mixing or sterilising and may be used
straight from the bag. It is very light, and being free-draining
there is less likelihood of overwatering this compost than with
some of the other media we have been using. It also retains
moisture well, and this too is an advantage for the gardener who
is not able to attend to his plants perhaps twice a day in hot
weather.

Some of the soilless composts we have used in the past have been
very difficult to wet again if they have been allowed to dry out;
in fact the only way to do this has been to submerge the pot in a
bucket of water for a time. The new compost, however, if it should
dry out should be watered thoroughly, left for an hour or so, and
then watered again. The compost comes in two types, the potting
compost and the seedling compost. The seedling compost may be
used in pots or boxes for seed sowing, and for rooting cuttings. It
is not necessary to cover fine seeds such as lobelia and similar
plants at all; they are just sown on the surface of the compost,
which has already been thoroughly watered and allowed to drain,

and then a sheet of glass covered with paper is placed over the top of the pots or boxes. I find that the green polythene sheeting used by many gardeners for greenhouse blinds is excellent for covering pots or boxes of newly sown seeds. It cuts out much of the radiated sun heat, and prevents too rapid drying-out of the compost. Larger seeds are just lightly covered with the compost, which is pressed level with a piece of wood.

The potting compost is used for pricking out seedlings and for potting plants of all sizes. When pricking out or potting in this compost it is not necessary or desirable to firm the seedlings or plants. A thorough watering after they have been inserted in the compost is sufficient to settle the soil around them, and the open texture of the compost permits rapid root action.

On the subject of growing plants in pots, either in the greenhouse or indoors, it may be worth pointing out that the idea which some people have that plants should be repotted every year is not always correct. Most plants should go two, if not three years in the same pot, provided they have been put into a large enough pot at the last potting, and that they have been intelligently and regularly fed. One should only feed plants when they are making growth, and this means as a rule that the feeding of house plants should decrease about the end of September. Plants that are still growing such as cinerarias, cyclamen, and so on, chrysanthemums, primulas, and other plants that will flower in the winter or early part of the year, can continue to receive regular feeding.

In general it is usually better to feed little and often; by that I mean putting on an application of liquid fertiliser diluted according to the makers' instructions but using it at half strength twice as frequently as it is recommended to be used at full strength. Naturally the old clever growers who are aiming at show perfection have their own special favourites in mixtures of fertilisers, but those of us who only wish to produce reasonably good results need not concern ourselves with these niceties. There are plenty of good fertilisers on the market especially compounded for pot plants and these, used intelligently, nearly always give satisfactory results.

Worm worries

WHENEVER I mention worms on the lawn, and suggest that we should get rid of them if possible, I always know that some people will write either to say that worms are useful in the lawn, or that chemical treatment of lawns to eradicate worms is dangerous to birds who may pick up a treated worm and be affected by the chemical it has consumed.

Certainly there are worms that work away in the soil and do not produce unsightly wormcasts. In cultivated ground there is no problem, but if we want good turf we do not want worm casts on it; they have to be swept off before the grass is cut, and an accidental tread on a wormcast allows weed seeds, blown on to it, to germinate very quickly, or moss eventually to penetrate it.

The new Rentokil wormkiller is based upon the carbamate insecticide Carbaryl. The makers claim that results are visible within four days; the worms die underground, and one treatment will last a whole season. They also say it is harmless to birds. It is now that casting worms feed near the surface, and treatment either now or in the spring, another feeding period, should be effective. This wormkiller also controls leatherjackets and wireworms. In my own lawns I do not have many problems with wireworms, but from time to time leatherjackets do damage the turf. The wormkiller is watered on through a fine-rosed watering can, two gallons to each six square yards, costing about 1*d* a square yard.

This is the time to apply a good organic autumn turf conditioner. We do not want quick-acting fertilisers at this time, but something that will last well and tone the grass up in time for next season.

Also a good raking with a wire rake just now, to remove dead grass and other rubbish, is well worth while. This is especially necessary if one has been cutting the grass during dry spells without the mower box on. A thorough raking, and dealing with minor humps and hollows, will probably do more than anything to improve the look of your lawn.

There are now special hollow-tined tools which take out cores of soil, and the minor bumps can be levelled by spiking them in this way, then rolling them a little, repeating the treatment until they are level with the rest of the lawn. Large humps, of course, have to be treated by slitting the grass, folding it back, and removing a little soil. Minor hollows can be filled in gradually by several dressings of sifted soil, just sufficient to hide the grass, and well brushed in. This smoothing up process greatly enhances a lawn's appearance.

The campanulas

I WAS reflecting recently on the enormous variety and usefulness of the bell flower family, that great genus *Campanula* of which over 250 wild species are known, all from the northern hemisphere strangely. It is perhaps unusual that this large genus, which varies so enormously – some plants are dwarf and creeping, others grow up to 6 ft – with very few exceptions produces little colour variation. The majority are blue, but of course there are many white forms known. The Canterbury Bell, a native of southern Europe, does give a wide colour range, blue, violet, white, pink, and with its either double or cup-and-saucer flowers offers considerable variation in form.

Among the types of campanulas suitable for herbaceous beds or borders, some progress has been made in producing colour variations, mainly in shades of blue and violet, but *Campanula lactiflora* 'Loddon Anna', which grows about 3 or 4 ft, has broken new ground with a flesh-pink flower.

Other varieties of this handsome campanula include the dwarf nine-inch 'Pouffe' which makes a mound of light blue flowers, and there are variations of light blue in the species itself, which grows to about three feet.

An imperturbable campanula is *C. glomerata* and its varieties *dahurica* with violet-purple flowers, *nana alba* or 'Purple Pixie', violet-purple, and these are all well worth planting either in mixed collections of herbaceous plants or in a fairly bold group on their own in any odd corner where something which will look after itself is required. Incidentally, the tall varieties which include *C. latiloba* 'Percy Piper' with deep blue flowers, have the advantage that they need no support. With the peach-leaved campanulas, varieties of *C. persicifolia*, either single or double, I find it necessary to use a few twiggy sticks early on because they do tend to flop around a little, especially after heavy rain.

A little-known campanula, growing to about 18 in. is *C. alliariifolia* 'Ivory Bells'. It comes from the Caucasus and has hairy leaves with graceful arching stems carrying large white flowers. Most campanulas naturally are perennial, but the Chimney Bell flower, *C. pyramidalis*, is biennial and makes an excellent pot plant for bringing into a large hall, where its 4 or 5 ft of flower stems will be much admired. It needs the protection of a frame in winter.

For the rock-garden-plant enthusiasts, the family is both a joy and a despair, for some of the most attractive campanulas are not easy to grow and are consequently somewhat rare. Botanists have had quite a time with the names of the various species, and when they have made their inevitable name changes, I feel they have not always changed for the better as far as the gardener is concerned.

For example, that delightful rich purple, low-growing species which we used to know as *C. muralis*, and which is so right for growing in the chinks of a flat stone wall or between two stones in the rock garden, must now be known as *C. portenschlagiana*. Then I always thought that *C. pusilla* was a charming name for the graceful little plant which only grows three or four inches high and cheerfully carpets quite a large area with its bright blue flowers; it is now officially *C. cochlearifolia*, a name which means little to us gardeners.

Most campanulas are easily raised from seed; indeed Thompson
& Morgan (Ipswich) Ltd, list over sixty species and varieties. The
dwarfer alpine varieties, however, are usually reproduced by
cuttings, although some may be increased by dividing the clumps
into small pieces. I much prefer to do propagating in the spring,
and with cuttings or divisions it is wise to keep them in a cold
frame until they have made decent sized plants for putting out.

Tracing the unusual plant

MINE is a perpetual dilemma. If I recommend only plants that
are widely distributed in the trade, I may be accused of lacking
knowledge and imagination. If I recommend plants which are
rare or even fairly scarce, it tends to irritate the reader because
he does not know where to buy them. Naturally, if I mention a
plant I always check that it is available somewhere, and I am
always happy to indicate a source or sources of supply. But of
course I am not in a position to know all the nurseries that stock
any particular plant, and sometimes I have to recommend the
reader to a firm many miles away from his home. If he orders
from this firm, the plants have to be sent by road or rail, and they
often take a long time to reach their destination. Also, freight
charges today are fairly high.

So I welcomed the news that the Horticultural Trades
Association has established a 'plant finder' service. Anyone
wishing to trace a source of supply of a rare, unusual, or new plant
may write direct to the Plant Finder Service, The Horticultural
Trades Association, 6th Floor, Cereal House, Mark Lane,
London, E.C.3. A reply can be expected within two or three days,
but where particularly rare or uncommon plants are sought, it
may take two or three weeks to find a supplier.

This is an excellent idea and should give much more scope to
recommend plants which, because they are little known, have not

been much in demand and have therefore not been propagated in any quantity. But I can see that for some time the exercise of a more liberal policy in the recommendation of unusual plants may have a kind of self-cancelling effect. By publicising them, the demand will soon soak up existing stocks, as happened when I mentioned the lovely pink thornless climbing rose 'Zephirine Drouhin'. The small stocks up and down the country were soon exhausted. The new plant finder service should, I hope, encourage the nurserymen to propagate more of the lesser-known plants if the demand justifies it. The service may help to reverse the trend towards streamlining the lists of available plants.

I can think of many plants that should be far more widely grown, and would be if only they were more freely available. Magnolias, for example, have been in such short supply that one hesitated to recommend them even though in many small nurseries small stocks of the different species were known to exist.

Some years ago, camellias were scarce. Now there are large stocks in nurseries – perhaps because nobody wrote about them for several years, or maybe because some gardeners bought camellias and lost them during their first winter, and discouraged their friends from buying them. It is of the utmost importance to protect the roots of a young camellia from frost during the first few years after planting. If the roots of a camellia are frozen, it will die. So one must put a foot-thick layer of leaves, straw, peat, or similar material around the plants every autumn until they have penetrated deeply enough to be out of reach of frost. If you have an acid soil, a semi-shaded spot where the early morning sun does not reach the flowers, or a north wall, camellias are well worth planting. They grow slowly certainly, but they will last at least one lifetime.

The lovely blue-flowered climber *Solanum crispum* is a fine wall plant, and in my father's garden in the middle of Hyde Park reached well above his bedroom window. Then *Cytisus battandieri* which carries golden 'candles' vertically along its branches, is another small tree which would grace any garden. It also has very attractive silvery leaves.

Another little-known plant is *Crocosmia masonorum*, but it is infinitely well worth growing. It resembles a montbretia but is smaller and has brilliant scarlet flowers. In my experience it is wise to cover the roots in winter with a layer of peat or leaves, as I have lost one or two plants, I think, through frost over the years.

Somewhat similar in its habits – sword-like leaves and orange-red flowers – is *Antholyza paniculata major*, familiarly known as Auntie Liza. This is an extremely vigorous plant, given reasonably moist and rich ground. It normally grows to about three feet high, but in a north border behind a wall, fairly shaded, it grows even taller with me.

Many gardeners grow a plant or two of the blue agapanthus in tubs which they keep in a greenhouse in winter and put outside in summer. But they do not realise that there are several of these handsome plants that may be grown outdoors. The latest are the 'Headbourne' hybrids. There are also the dwarf blue *A. mooreanus minus*, and the rich blue *A. weillighii*, but this is a scarce plant.

Jobs for September

OUTDOOR chrysanthemums and dahlias need regular attention to tying, pest and disease control, and disbudding, if large flowers are required. Watch carefully for any signs of virus disease on these plants – misshapen flowers, mottled leaves, prominent yellowing round the veins on the leaves, anything abnormal. Mark these plants for destruction after flowering. If there are many affected plants, resolve to destroy the lot and make a fresh start.

Prune climbing and rambler roses. With ramblers there are usually plenty of new stems every year so one can cut out to ground level all those that flowered this year. Tie in the new growths to take their place. Climbing roses are usually less free with their new growths, and it is not usually possible to do more than cut out a few of the oldest growths and tie in the new ones.

But with both types of rose, try to bend the stems over into a semi-circle or as nearly horizontal as possible to promote the production of flowering side shoots.

Remove all suckers from bush roses, lilacs or rhododendrons: cut them off below ground at the point where they leave the roots.

Keep on spraying roses, michaelmas daisies and other plants that are prone to mildew. There is still time to water weeds on lawns with a selective weedkiller, and if moss is present kill it with a mercuric moss-killer.

Order bulbs now, both for growing in bowls and for planting outdoors.

Prepare planting sites for new roses, trees, shrubs, and fruit trees or bushes.

Cut back any shrubs or perennial evergreen rock plants that are overcrowding their neighbours.

Give all the fruit trees and bushes a dressing of a proprietary fertiliser.

Finish all the hedge trimming as soon as possible.

Hurry now to sow a new lawn if this is to be done this autumn, or if there are bare patches, scratch up the surface and sow seed in the next week or two.

October

If truth were told October should be the start of the gardener's year. Certainly the autumn leaves and berries and the last of the summer flowers will give us pleasure for a few weeks yet, but we must be hard hearted, remove the summer bedding and replace it with the flowers of spring.

Usually October and the first week or two of November are open enough for us to press on with clearing up and preparing sites for new plantings. These are usually the last weeks when the weather is really inviting enough to entice us away from the fireside and the television – we should make the most of them. Also new plantings made before the soil becomes cold will take root and thrive better than those delayed until later in the year or in the spring. The prudent gardener, especially if he lives on heavy clay, will press on hard and hurry with the work.

Renovating the borders

IN theory the border of hardy herbaceous flowers should be labour-saving and a joy for at least six months of the year. In fact, the traditional border looks fine from about the end of May until about the middle of July, and then it begins to look tatty. Furthermore, the old-fashioned type of border backed by a hedge or a wall needs a great deal of attention in the way of staking, because the plants tend to become drawn.

The modern way of growing hardy herbaceous flowers in irregular-shaped beds in the open has much to commend it. Unless the garden is in a very windy position, there are many hardy flowers that can be grown in these free-standing beds and will need no support.

Many of us are saddled with herbaceous borders backing on to a wall or hedge, and it may be rather a major operation to move them. But if there is sufficient room in the garden the borders could be emptied and new beds made several feet away from the wall or fence and the plants replanted in a much more informal manner.

In theory a border of hardy flowers should be renovated every four or five years. In fact, these borders can be left for ten or twelve years but inevitably the soil becomes impoverished, the better plants tend to die out, the strong-growing plants, usually of rather poor varieties, spread, and there comes a time when the whole thing must be taken apart and replanted. This is a very good time of the year to embark on such a major operation. All the poor types of michaelmas daisies, for example, should be thrown away. There are many plants, no doubt, in every border that do not pay for their keep. These may be discarded.

Once the border is emptied it should be dug through conscientiously and all roots of perennial weeds or the types of michaelmas daisies that run for yards should be removed. Plenty

of dung or hop manure should be dug in and the border made
ready for replanting.

Planting can be done in the autumn or in the spring, but my
own preference is to plant those plants that have long tap roots,
such as lupins and anchusas, in the autumn, and the fibrous-
rooted plants – the phloxes and michaelmas daisies, the erigerons
and geums – in March.

Choosing the plants for an herbaceous border or for informal
beds is not easy. One may wish to have a glorious blaze of colour
in June and July or, if these beds are in full view of the windows
of the house, some colour for many months. The choice of plants
is obviously a matter of personal preference. There are now so
many varieties of lupins, delphiniums, michaelmas daisies, irises
and day lilies, varieties of hemerocallis, that I do not propose to
offer suggestions, but I would like to suggest a few plants that
could be fitted into any herbaceous border or free-standing bed.

To start the flowering season in April there are the varieties of
doronicum, those lovely single yellow daisy flowers which,
incidentally, are also good for cutting. There is *Doronicum* 'Miss
Mason' which grows to about 2 ft, *D. cordatum*, about 6 in. high,
or, if one likes double flowers, there is *D.* 'Spring Beauty', about
18 in. Flowering a little later are the bleeding hearts, varieties of
dicentra, and besides the old familiar *D. spectabilis* which really
needs a cool damp place, there are the varieties of *D. formosa*,
such as 'Adrian Bloom' with crimson flowers, and the white form
of *D. eximea*, known as 'Alba'.

Once we get into the month of June there are, of course, many
lovely hardy flowers. The erigerons suffer from no diseases and
few pests, they flower for many months and, given perhaps the
support of a few pea sticks, are beautiful and trouble-free. They
come nowadays in many colours, lilac-pink, violet-blue, rosy
lavender, rose pink and violet-mauve.

Surprisingly one seldom sees *Galtonia candicans*, which grows to
about 3 ft and carries large white bell flowers. It is a robust hardy
plant and flowers profusely in July and August.

The hardy geraniums such as *G. endressii* 'A. T. Johnson' with silvery-pink flowers, or *G. wallichianum* 'Buxton's Blue' are easy to grow and flower for many weeks. Our horticultural ingenuity can be used to the full in choosing the plants that match up with each other and flower together.

It is important, however, to cater for the autumn. Plant such aconites as *Aconitum* 'Newry Blue' or 'Blue Sceptre', 3 ft and 2 ft high respectively; they need no support. Mixed with varieties of Japanese anemones, or the orange red hot poker, *Kniphofia galpinii*, they are charming in late summer and autumn.

Chinks, sinks and bottles

MANY gardening books are just a rehash of previous works on the same subject, sometimes with a little leaven of new ideas, but only too often the old mixture as before. Now and again an author turns up who breaks new ground, and Miss Anne Ashberry, who has published books on miniature gardens and on bottle gardens and fern cases, has now produced another quite original work on alpine lawns (*Alpine Lawns*, Hodder & Stoughton, 30s).

Now the alpine lawn may sound something rather exotic and beyond the reach of the ordinary gardener, but in these days when we are all looking for ways of reducing maintenance costs, the ideas that Anne Ashberry offers could be most helpful. The alpine lawn, it must be said at once, is not something that you walk over. You could perhaps walk over it occasionally with little damage, as you might walk over some lower reaches of an alp in Switzerland; but the alpine lawn is not something that will support frequent pedestrian traffic.

The whole idea of the alpine lawn is to cover the ground with weed-smothering plants, such as heathers, thymes, chamomile, the mossy *Sagina* which we have to suffer in our lawns and usually exterminate ruthlessly, but which could be usefully employed on an area where it would not offend. Miss Ashberry remembers that

not everybody gardens in ideal country conditions, that many try
to embellish a backyard of a town house. She has kept these people
in mind, and has even sketched out a planting plan for a garden
made of old bricks laid edge to edge, and for a roof garden.

Naturally when she moves on to the less inhibiting sites in
country gardens she is able to let her imagination romp away, and
many suggestions are offered for carpeting large areas with attractive and virtually trouble-free plants.

Miss Ashberry also devotes part of her book to plants that love
to grow in crevices in walls. This is a very interesting side alley
of gardening, because many plants that one could not make happy
on the flat, on soils that are perhaps rather poorly drained, can be
grown to perfection in crevices of flat stone walls. In the Munich
Botanic Garden there is a wonderful long bed built of flat stone
walls with earth between the stones, and on the top an ordinary
bed of soil. On the north side of this wall grow ramondas and
many other plants that do not like full sun, and on the other side
are many of the sun-loving alpine plants that revel in this quick-
draining position. On the top, which is also freely drained, there
is a collection of alpine plants that would make a rock-garden
lover's mouth water in this country.

Miss Ashberry's book on bottle gardens, which appeared some
two years ago, has stimulated many people to grow plants in cider
'pottles', carboys, and other containers. My eldest daughter
became quite enthused by this book and planted several carboys
and bottles for friends. To her chagrin, most of her first efforts
failed because, as we now know, she made the compost too wet
to begin with. You would think that by leaving the neck of the
bottle open, uncorked, any surplus moisture would soon evaporate,
but apparently this does not happen. The atmosphere inside is too
humid, and most of the plants rotted. So during her Christmas
holidays she started again with several carboys, put in the layer
of charcoal at the bottom, followed by some pebbles – an inch of
each – then an inch of peat, and two or three inches of John Innes
compost No. 3, and replanted them. She kept the compost
on the dry side, working on the principle that one can always

add water if necessary. The results have been most satisfactory.

If anyone wishes to experiment with bottle gardens I suggest that they are planted with the minimum of moisture in the compost. If the plants show any sign of distress a little water can be added, but this must be done judiciously.

And the would-be carboy gardener should hurry up because manufacturers are now sending their chemicals out in plastic containers, and it looks as if the glass carboy and the glass beer bottle will be something the next generation will see only in museums. If one had the storage space, it might be a worth-while investment to lay away a few dozen carboys: after all, it is only a few years ago that stone sinks could be picked up for practically nothing, and now they are fetching high prices.

My wife and I have become very fond of miniature roses. There are now many varieties to choose from and we find that they go on flowering for a long time. They are exceedingly easy to manage, although naturally you have to keep a sharp watch for aphis and caterpillars because the miniatures are just as susceptible to damage from these pests as their larger brothers and sisters.

Rock garden plant purists look askance at miniature roses in a rock garden, but if you do not wish to lay claim to being an alpine-plant lover there is no reason why a rock garden should not contain a few of these beautiful little modern miniatures. I have found that miniature roses also thrive very happily in stone sinks, tubs, window boxes and similar containers. One tends to forget that they need feeding now and then, but if they are pruned really hard in December – cut the stems back to leave about 2 to 3 in. – they flower freely and keep neat and shapely.

The pieces removed may be used as cuttings as they root quite easily. Pieces about 6 in. long are inserted to about half their length in a pot of ordinary seed sowing compost, or even in a shallow trench lined with sand in a sheltered spot in the garden. The base of the stem will form a knobbly callus during the winter, and will probably thrust out roots about May. Then next autumn, if it is in the open garden, it may be lifted and planted in the rock garden or wherever it may be desired to grow. Those rooted in pots may be planted as soon as they have made plenty of roots. They grow quite well on their own roots, as indeed do practically all of the modern roses. If they are not so vigorous on their own roots as plants budded on the briar understock, this does not really matter in a rock garden or in a stone sink – indeed it can be an advantage. In the north pruning should be delayed until late March or April.

Troubles that are always with us

PESTS and diseases are always with us, but one can become quite hypochondriacal about them. Some pests we shall always have – greenfly, for example, the worst pest in British gardens after the bullfinches. Caterpillars at certain times can be a menace but there are plenty of insecticides that will take care of these, if they are applied regularly and early enough to prevent a massive build-up.

At the present time, moss is usually appearing in many lawns. It should be dealt with smartly now, by watering on a mercuric moss-killer which can be obtained from any good garden shop. This kills the moss immediately and there is no need to rake it out. If the moss is left to grow it will do so lustily throughout the winter because moss, unlike grass, can grow during the low-light conditions of the British winter.

Another intractable problem in the garden is that of canker in fruit trees – apples and pears. Branches that are attacked by this disease become gnarled and soon die. All cankered branches must be cut out and the cut surfaces painted with one of the special compounds made for sealing tree wounds. Brown rot on fruits of apples, pears and quinces is another problem that presents itself every year, and here again prophylactic measures are indicated. All brown or mummified fruits should be gathered up from the ground beneath the trees and picked off the branches, to be disposed of on the bonfire. If they are left lying about they will only produce more spores to infect the trees next year.

Mildew is always a problem and while it can be dealt with by spraying with a copper fungicide I prefer to side-step this particular trouble and remove varieties that are prone to the disease. The rose 'Fashion' is particularly susceptible, I find, in my garden, especially if it is planted in a corner where there is no through current of air to dry off the early morning dews. There are certain varieties of michaelmas daisy – unfortunately that magnificent red one 'Winston Churchill' – which are more prone to mildew than others. Nobody wants to conduct a kind of horticultural convalescent home in his garden and it pays to be ruthless and eliminate all plants that year after year require constant spraying to keep them in good health.

A fairly frequent inquiry concerns the question of lopping trees that have become too large for their position. Often fruit trees or ornamental trees have been planted too near a wall or a fence. There comes a time when they must be lopped. Lilacs, for example, often grow tall and leggy and these can be cut down to 2 ft or 3 ft above ground and will branch out again. With large fruit trees, however, it is better to do the lopping by easy stages. Half the branches could be lopped this year and the other half next autumn.

Another problem that often arises is the possibility of damage to the foundations of the house through the roots of trees. Poplars are the main offenders; their roots can travel as much as fifty yards and still cause damage to the foundations of buildings. The damage is usually serious only in clay soils but if there are poplars near a building it would be wise to dig down 2 ft or 3 ft deep to see whether the roots are menacing the foundations. Several legal actions have been brought when the roots of poplar trees have damaged buildings, and substantial damages have been awarded against the unlucky owners of the poplars.

The weeping willow is less of a menace than the poplar, but it should never be planted in a small garden or even in a large garden on light quick-draining soil. A large weeping willow can transpire vast quantities of moisture through its leaves and its roots can rob the soil for many yards around. Naturally, if the soil is heavy, retentive and possibly lying a little wet, a weeping willow can perform a very useful function by removing excess moisture from the ground.

We must now expect field mice to come indoors and to penetrate frames and greenhouses, where they can cause much damage. For many years I trapped mice by baiting with a melon seed but I have now discovered that a small piece of milk chocolate is even better.

Any day now we shall be lifting our gladioli and dahlias and here again we should be ruthless in destroying any plants that show signs of abnormality – mottled or withered foliage which could be caused by virus disease or some other trouble. The affected plants should be destroyed.

If these lines have made dismal reading, I apologise, but in gardening we must be always vigilant and side-step trouble whenever possible.

Equable pot plants

As winter draws nearer and cut flowers become more expensive, many people turn to pot plants, either flowering or with attractive foliage, as these represent excellent value. One learns by experience which kinds of plant will survive the conditions of the home and the care – or lack of it – they are likely to receive.

Human nature being what it is, the easier the plant is to grow, and the more long-suffering it is over sporadic watering, dust on the leaves, inadequate feeding, stuffy atmosphere, wide fluctuations in temperature, draughts, and other hazards, the less attention it tends to get from many people.

However, when choosing a plant to give to a friend it is necessary to proceed with care. Some people are notorious plant killers, and it is a waste of time giving them anything less tough than a sansevieria. Others can perform wonders in growing plants that are classified by the grower as intermediate or even delicate.

Much depends on the conditions in the recipient's home – a steady background heat of around 18° C (65° F) suits most plants, but too dry an atmosphere is hard on them. Cyclamen will often last in flower for months in a cool room, or in the entrance hall where the temperature would range between 55° F or 60° F. The silvery-leaved cyclamen have proved more able to withstand living-room conditions than the older green-leaved type. These are the varieties to look for when buying cyclamen.

One of the easiest is the rubber plant, *Ficus decora*, but it soon becomes too large for a small room and has to be cut back. There are now good stocks of *F. robusta* which has shorter joints between the leaves and makes a shapely plant even in a $3\frac{1}{2}$ in. pot.

The tradescantias are justly popular as they are able to thrive in most living rooms. The variegated forms tend to revert to the normal green colour when the plants become old. The new variety 'Quicksilver', with its green and silvery leaves, is much more stable in this respect. Extremely long-suffering is *Chlorophytum capense*, with its long, narrow, green and yellow striped leaves. It is popular as an office plant because it does not mind being left unwatered over the weekend. All the ivies are easy, and so is *Hoya carnosa* with its heads of waxy white flowers. The hoya looks as though it would not be happy indoors, but it is no problem. The peperomias, *Philodendron scandens*, *Rhoicissus rhomboidea*, *Sedum sieboldii*, and *Cissus antarctica* are all easy to grow.

Moving on to others that are more difficult to keep happy indefinitely in the home, there are the saintpaulias. Many people succeed if the plants are stood on one of the special plastic trays filled with pebbles and water, and kept in a steady room temperature. The supply in the shops during winter is erratic as the growers do not send them out except during mild spells.

The 'Calamondin' oranges are an engaging novelty when they are well set with their miniature oranges; some people like to have a plant by their cocktail cabinet, so that they can pick a fruit to slice off a 'zest' for the cocktails. But like most of the intermediate and the delicate types of plant, it really needs to go to a greenhouse or conservatory for a period of rehabilitation after a spell indoors.

The handsome 'Mikkelsen' poinsettias will be making their appearance in the shops again, as the growers prepare an early batch for the Jewish New Year. These remarkable poinsettias survive for many weeks, given reasonably cool conditions and careful watering. Besides the red, pink, and white varieties, there is now 'Mikkeldawn' with pink and white flowers. These, too, need to go into a greenhouse after flowering, or be looked on as expendable. Even so, they are excellent value because they last so long.

One of the most equable of all house plants is *Clivia miniata*, with its huge heads of orange flowers that last for weeks indoors. It may be stood outside all summer and brought in again before the autumn frosts.

You never tire of trees

IN the concluding paragraph of *Landscape with Trees* (Country Life, £3 3s) the author, Miles Hadfield, quotes Lord Beaconsfield's observation: 'You may tire of mountains and rivers, you may tire of the sea, but you can never tire of trees.' Anyone who has the slightest feeling for the British landscape, and for trees, would agree, and would find fascinating Mr Hadfield's account of the part trees played in forming our scenery.

From just after the Ice Age until now, the history of our trees has been one of natural or man-created hazards, lack of foresight, official procrastination and dithering, the crippling effect of wars on the forests, and so on. That the country now pursues a more enlightened policy over forests is to be applauded, but as the author says, there seems little doubt that a world timber shortage is round the corner, and this is not the time to relax our replanting programme.

Even if one is not personally concerned with the problems of afforestation or forest maintenance, this is a delightful book.

Most of us, however, cannot plant trees on a grand scale, and as gardens are inevitably becoming smaller we have to concentrate on the smaller, shorter-lived ornamental trees, cherries, laburnums and the like. More people, however, could plant such slow-growing trees as the quince – always a good cropper in my garden – which flowers late and usually escapes the frosts. Then if only there were an adequate supply of mulberries we might see more of these very long-lived, but slow-growing trees, which are so adaptable and impervious to the adverse conditions of towns.

I must confess that the shortage of mulberry trees in the trade baffles me. They are fairly easily propagated, indeed quite large pieces of branch will root, and with modern methods I should have thought stocks could be worked up fairly quickly. Certainly there would be a demand if plants were available.

It is puzzling too, that training topiary specimens of yew and box seems to have died out in this country. There are specimens available, but these are imported from the Continent. Perhaps labour costs or shortage of labour have caused this small industry to die out here, but I would hardly have thought that continental growers were any better placed than we are. Anyone with the time to spare and the patience to train topiary specimens should find it worth while.

While talking of box, one must remember that these bushes, with very dense foliage that throws off the rain, often suffer from lack of moisture at the roots, while other plants are perfectly happy. So in dry spells it is wise to remember the box bushes, and give them a little extra water.

Jobs for October

HARDEN your heart and remove summer bedding plants if these are to be replaced by wallflowers, myosotis, tulips, daffodils, or other spring-flowering plants. It may seem a trifle obvious to suggest that the wallflowers should be planted first, and the tulip bulbs afterwards, but more than once I have seen a jobbing gardener do it the other way round and bring up dozens of tulip bulbs, sliced in half on his trowel.

If bedded out, begonias have to be lifted while they are still in full leaf, put in boxes of soil in a greenhouse and the stems allowed to die back gradually.

Lift gladioli, tie them in small bundles of a dozen or so, and hang them in an airy shed to dry off.

If there are worm casts on the lawn, sweep them off before mowing, and treat the lawn with one of the proprietary wormkillers.

If you want a lawn to be proud of next year, rake out all the dead grass and other debris now with a wire rake. If you still have the energy, spike the lawn with a garden fork, making holes 4 to 6 in. deep about 4 in. apart, or do the same thing with a hollow-tined fork which removes cores of soil. Then brush in a good organic fertiliser, which all good garden shops can supply. If all this is too much trouble, just brush into the lawn the autumn fertiliser. With lawns you get what you work for – but to have a perfect lawn you have to put in a lot of work. There is still just time to apply a selective weedkiller, and if there is moss in the lawn, a mercuric moss-killer applied now will kill it and prevent an alarming infestation, because moss grows all winter when the grass is pretty well dormant.

Plant bulbs in bowls or pots. The pre-cooled daffodils and tulips, and the prepared hyacinths, which you can have in flower by Christmas, should be planted early in the month. Ordinary bulbs, not specially treated, and which will flower in the new year, should also be planted in the next week or two. Daffodils and all the small bulbs for outdoors are best planted in October. Tulips can wait if need be for another month or more.

If you have a small pool, spread a net over it to catch falling leaves. They pollute the water and may harm the fish if the pool is frozen over, as they give off poisonous gases in decay. This idea of spreading a net over the pool can also be applied to the rock garden. It is so much easier to lift off the net than to grub about picking the leaves out from among the rock plants.

Lift geraniums, fuchsias, and other tender plants and pot them up. Bring in cyclamen, azaleas, or similar plants that have been standing outside for the summer. We may not have a frost for weeks yet but is better to be safe than sorry.

Check gutters and surface drain covers. Leaves can choke them and cause minor, but sometimes annoying floods.

Mark with a cane and a label every herbaceous plant that you intend to remove or lift and divide. When the stems die down it is difficult to be sure which plants you intended to deal with.

If you have ordered trees, shrubs, rose bushes, or the like, prepare the ground for them now. Dig it over, loosen the subsoil, and work in compost, well-decayed manure, hop manure, mushroom compost, or even peat and bone meal – a double handful of bone meal to a bucketful of moist peat. Never dig in dry peat.

November

November can be a miserable month with the ever-present risk of fog and frost. The carpet of leaves has to be gathered up, the debris of the summer crops has to be removed. The birds are now turning a beady eye towards the buds on our fruit trees. The season is over. But if the weather is reasonable and one has the moving spirit a concentrated effort to have the garden tidied up by the end of the year pays off handsomely. Then if the weather should close in on us after Christmas, we can sit back in the smug knowledge that there is not a huge backload of work to be done in the spring.

Reliable herbaceous plants

A FRIEND, anxious to replant a fairly large herbaceous border, asked me to mark a catalogue for him, and it may be that the suggestions I made for him will be of interest. He already had several phloxes which he proposed to divide up, but I suggested one or two more, because phloxes are indeed excellent value, flowering as they do for a long period.

He had raised from seed a selection of lupins which flowered for the first time last year, and he had marked all the interesting colours for removal to the border in due course. Sundry other fairly common plants, such as erigerons and rudbeckias, he proposed to keep from the old border, and divide up, so these are not included in the list I marked for him. One rudbeckia, however, 'Robert Bloom', an orange-centred, carmine-purple flower, I recommended because it is quite outstanding.

To save time searching through catalogues, I propose to group the plants recommended into their heights – the first selection would be for the front of the border, the second group for the middle, and the taller ones for the back. Ideally one should have a herbaceous bed or border free-standing, away from walls or fences, with the taller plants in the middle and the lower growing plants on either side. Planted like this away in the open, they need little in the way of support because they will not be drawn towards the light as they would be when planted against a wall or hedge.

Seldom grown today, but always interesting, is the Prophet's Flower, *Arnebia echioides*, with yellow flowers and black spots. The dwarf michaelmas daisies are excellent value, and here I would recommend 'Audrey', mauve-blue, 'Jenny', violet-purple, and 'Snowsprite', white.

Many people hesitate to grow astilbes because they feel they need moist conditions which they cannot provide, but in Munich

Botanic Gardens are some of the finest astilbes I have ever seen, growing in rather arid woodland conditions, but as they are assiduously watered they succeed magnificently. I would recommend *Astilbe* 'Bressingham Beauty', rich pink, 'Fanal', deep red, *A. glaberrima saxosa*, a dwarf pink variety 6 in. high, and *A. simplicifolia* 'Bronze Elegance', with dark leaves and pink flowers about a foot high. A little known plant but very good natured is *Baptisia australis exaltata* which makes a lovely bush about 2 ft 6 in. high with dark blue flowers.

Of campanulas there is a wide choice, but I would recommend *C.* 'Purple Pixie' with violet-purple flowers in late summer, *C. persicifolia* 'Blue Belle', and *C. trachelium* 'Bernice'.

The pink chicory, *Chicorum intybus roseum*, is worth growing; and of the moon daisies, varieties of *Chrysanthemum maximum*, I would settle for 'Wirral Supreme', double white.

The border clematis are fun, and *C.* 'Crepuscule', lavender blue, and *C. recta grandiflora* with scented white flowers are excellent.

The orange *Crocosmia masonorum*, which flowers late – in August or September – is a marvellous flower either for the border or for cutting, and should be in every garden. Leaving aside the tall delphiniums, one should always include one or two of the Belladonna varieties, and *D. ruysii* 'Pink Sensation' or the gentian blue 'Wendy' would be a good choice.

For border pinks there is a wide selection but 'Brympton Red', 'Excelsior', a pink form of 'Mrs Sinkins', and the double white 'White Ladies' would do well in the front of any border.

An unusual foxglove is *Digitalis ambigua* with yellow flowers. If you yearn to have gentians in the garden, even if it is on alkaline soil, *G. hascombensis* is a good one to choose.

Christmas roses one should have, and *Helleborus niger* 'Potter's Wheel' is the largest on offer today.

Unusual and always interesting are the incarvilleas, such as *I. delavayi* or *I.* 'Bees Pink'. The dwarf red hot pokers, such as *Kniphofia galpinii*, soft yellow, or *K. nelsonii major*, orange flame, would look well planted near *Liatris* 'Kobold' with deep lilac flowers. The perennial flax, *Linum narbonense*, clear blue, or the low-growing evening primrose, *Oenothera macrocarpa*, with enormous yellow flowers, would make a good neighbour for *Phygelius capensis coccineus*.

Some of the border varieties of potentilla are worth growing – 'Gibson's Scarlet' and 'Monsieur Rouillard', with huge crimson double flowers with an orange blotch. The Kaffir lilies, varieties of *Schizostylis*, flower late and can be had in either pink or red forms; and if one wants a dwarf thalictrum, *T. diffusiforme* with large mauve flowers is a good one to choose.

Turning to the plants for the second row, there are some wonderful aconites that give us blue flowers late in the year, *Aconitum arendsii* and *Aconitum* 'Blue Sceptre' with blue and white flowers; the *Alstroemeria* 'Ligtu Hybrids', in various colours, superb for cutting; Japanese anemones, of which my own favourites are 'Bressingham Glow', semi-double ruby-rose, 'Lady Gilmour', double pink and 'Louise Uhink', white; and *Antholyza paniculata major*, with orange-red montbretia-like flowers. Of the tall-growing michaelmas daisies a selection is a matter of personal preference but I would not like to be without 'Ernest Ballard', rosy-crimson, 'Marie Ballard', light blue, 'Mistress Quickly', dark blue, and 'Picture', carmine.

The campanulas come back here again with *C. lactiflora* 'Loddon Anna'. Of the taller red hot pokers the pale primrose variety 'Maid of Orleans' is excellent for the warmer part of the country, but I would not grow it north of the Midlands. For a traditional red hot poker 'Royal Standard' is a good choice. The tree mallow, *Lavatera olbia rosea*, with large pink flowers, will go on for years, and the bergamots, varieties of *Monarda*, are always worth growing.

The perennial scabious should appear in every border, and here 'Bressingham White' and 'Clive Greaves', the old favourite deep blue variety, take a lot of beating, and the taller verbascums such as 'Cotswold Beauty' and 'Gainsborough' are interesting even when they are not in flower because their grey foliage is always attractive.

My list of taller plants is limited, because one does not need too many of these in the garden. I should perhaps point out that in practically all hardy plant catalogues one should take the suggested heights with a pinch of salt because all hardy flowers tend to grow slightly taller in the rather shaded confines of a garden than they do in an open field. But for the middle of the border, or at the back, if that is the kind of border you have to plant, the creamy yellow *Aconitum lycoctonum*, the large-flowered varieties of delphinium such as 'Blackmore's Glorious', the white 'Swan Lake', or indeed any of the modern varieties; *Helenium* 'Spatrot', bronzy-red, *Helianthus* 'Loddon Gold', or even taller, 'Monarch'; *Salvia turkestanica superba* and *Salvia argentea*; *Sidalcea* 'Croftway Red' or 'Wensleydale', rosy-red; and of course *Thalictrum dipterocarpum*, or its double variety 'Hewitt's Double' would be sure to please.

Foliage for arrangements

THE end of November is a thin month for the housewife. There is very little to pick in the garden for flower arrangements. It is between seasons. The *Primula malacoides* in the greenhouse are not yet ready. The chrysanthemums, late-rooted cuttings planted in the greenhouse border, are chosen to be in flower from mid-December over the Christmas and New Year period. A few streptocarpus in blue, mauve, and pink are really past their best. So my wife has to use her ingenuity and make arrangements mainly of foliage of various kinds, with just the odd rose bud. But the effect is charming.

Our young eucalyptus trees – *E. gunnii, E. niphophila, E. parvifolia, E. perriniana* – have now made sufficient growth to permit the judicious removal here and there of some foliage during the winter. It is, of course, most effective, and very long lasting. All the species and varieties we are growing are chosen for their hardiness – special strains which have come from really cold areas in their native land. Some long shoots of rosemary and sprays of the now russety 'fossil tree' *Metasequoia glyptostroboides*, some trails of the variegated honeysuckle *Lonicera japonica aureo-reticulata* are all pressed into service.

The greenhouse provides a touch of silver with some shoots of *Senecio cineraria.* A few sprays of the almost white *Prunus subhirtella autumnalis* complete the arrangement. Strangely the birds leave this cherry alone, but on the spring-flowering form and the weeping variety which also flowers in spring, they rob the buds without mercy.

The metasequoia is one of those rare deciduous conifers that should be planted more often. The price of this relatively new introduction has come down in recent years, and one can buy a young tree for around 20s. As it survived the Ice Age – at least a few did in China – it is hardly surprising that it is a long-suffering tree.

One of mine has had a chequered career. My father acquired it as one of the first seedlings ever raised in this country. When he died, the tree was about 8 ft high, growing lushly in his damp wood, its roots covered with sphagnum moss, and reaching into several little streams. We brought it to Hurtmore where the soil is light, very quick-draining, overlying Bargate stone about two or three feet below. It had to be moved twice, so in fourteen years it has only put on another 6 ft or so. But given a really moist situation it grows much faster. Russell Page, the international landscape architect, has used it to great effect in a swamp in one French garden. In this respect it resembles that other superb deciduous conifer *Taxodium distichum* but so far it has not adopted the taxodium's habit of pushing out knobbly surface roots.

At one time I used to view with suspicion any kind of variegated plant. In the years I spent in the seed trade, we always chopped out any plant that showed signs of variegation, as in most cases it was an indication of the presence of a virus disease. I was also hesitant about planting the 'bybloem' and 'bizarre' tulips, those lovely varieties with a wonderful range of stripes and flakings, because this condition was produced by the presence of a virus. But once, visiting the bulb research station at Lisse in Holland, the director, a wonderful man, Dr van Slogteren, showed me his own private collection of these varieties. These he kept prudently apart from the rest. Now of course there are many striped and flaked tulips which are not infected by a virus.

Eager for varieties of evergreen foliage in the garden, I am now collecting every type of variegated golden or silver plant I can find. In recent years we have planted and propagated the golden form of *Lonicera nitida* 'Baggesen's Gold'. We acquired the green and silver *Pittosporum tobira* 'Variegatum', which we grow in a greenhouse as, in common with its relations, it would not be hardy enough for the open garden in Surrey. If only we could grow pittosporum hedges as they do in the West Country, my wife's winter foliage problems would be solved. The golden *Elaeagnus pungens* 'Maculata' is a prolific plant, and one need not be hesitant about cutting a few sprays for the house. So, too, with *Euonymus radicans* and its silvery variety 'Variegata' if one wants some trailing shoots for an arrangement. The variegated hollies are most valuable, but one could wish they grew a little faster. My favourites are *Ilex aquifolium* 'Argentea Marginata' and *I. a.* 'Golden King'. Another long-suffering shrub is *Senecio laxifolius* – often listed, erroneously I fear, as *S. greyii*, which I am told is quite a scarce plant. But under either name this grey-leaved shrub gives us cheerful foliage and cutting material in summer and winter. If it grows too large for its lodgings or becomes a trifle gaunt, it may be cut back ruthlessly and will begin all over again.

The new rules

THIS is the time of year when committees of amateur horti-cultural societies begin to plan for next year's flower shows. There are many thousands of small shows all over the country and of course a schedule of classes has to be prepared. Anyone who has competed or judged at a local show will be familiar with the anomalies that have arisen because of a loosely-worded schedule – and many an acrimonious argument has arisen as a result. The

Royal Horticultural Society has issued a revised version of its invaluable *Horticultural Show Handbook* for the guidance of organisers, schedule makers, exhibitors and judges. It is available from the Royal Horticultural Society, Vincent Square, London, S.W.1, price 4s or by post 5s. It is important that show organisers should follow the suggestions in the booklet, and even more important, if they followed those in its predecessor, that they acquire the new edition. Significant changes have been made, and it could lead to more acrimony if exhibitors followed the old booklet's advice, or if they followed that of the new booklet while the organisers were still working with the old one.

Such knotty problems as the definition of an 'annual' and 'herbaceous plant', the confusion between 'distinct', 'similar' or 'dissimilar' varieties, the loose use of words 'should' and 'must', and the problems that can arise from the unthinking use of 'and' and 'or' are all concisely dealt with.

I have never had the honour of judging an amateur flower show on the Continent. I have, however, been a member of several international grand juries judging large combined groups at international shows where there have been no niceties of schedule wording to worry about. Even then, there have been frantic protests against the jury's decisions. I hardly like to think what happens at local shows. But probably Gallic logic, and the infinite precisions of the French language, see to it that there is no friction. Let us therefore use the results of the deep thought that has gone into the *Horticultural Show Handbook*.

Modern lilies

THE lovely hybrid lilies raised by Mr Jan de Graaf in Oregon, U.S.A., have proved very adaptable to British gardens. For the record, the 'Mid-Century' hybrids, of mixed parentage, have proved very successful, and perhaps the two most outstanding are 'Enchantment', a vivid red, and 'Destiny', lemon yellow. These lilies are very free flowering, but like most lilies take a year or two to settle down, so do not expect too much from them in their first season. Unlike many of the older lilies, which prefer to have their roots shaded by shrubs or other plants, these American hybrids seem to prefer an open position.

It is only in recent years that the long trumpet-shaped hybrids such as the curiously named white 'Black Dragon', the 'Emerald Strain' with a touch of green in the early stages of flowering, the yellow 'Golden Clarion Strain' or 'Green Dragon', a lovely white with green outside, have appeared in grower's lists.

All these I have grown successfully, even in borders that receive sun for only part of the day, but 'Destiny' and 'Enchantment' have certainly been happiest in a rather hot border at the base of the south-facing wall. Not that, from my few years' experience of growing them, I would suggest this is the best place for them; they would probably be happier in a slightly less arid spot, although with regular watering in dry spells they have done remarkably well.

As Mr M. J. Jefferson-Brown wisely remarks in his book *Modern Lilies* (Faber, 36s): 'Some lilies grow like weeds, some grow respectably with discreet and proper attention, but some are genuinely difficult.'

He goes on to blame the many shopkeepers who display lily bulbs dry, naked, and often bruised, with damaged outer scales, on the shop counters, for many an amateur's failure. As he points out, lily bulbs are never dormant, neither are they protected by a tough outer coat like many other bulbs. They have to be handled gently, preferably packed in moist peat, and this is the way they are treated by serious merchants.

The only lilies that 'grow like weeds' in my garden are the purple, pink and white forms of *Lilium martagon*. They seed themselves on my borders, and very grateful we are. They are not striking, of course, but they are attractive for weeks and fit in with the heterogeneous mixture of old-fashioned flowers we grow in the borders behind our old house. In any garden in town or country, *Lilium testaceum* and *L. regale* will flourish. The tiger lilies, or *L. chalcedonicum* and, provided it is given a raised bed, or planted on a bank, the golden-rayed lily of Japan, *Lilium auratum*, will flourish.

But the more sophisticated lilies are flowers for the connoisseur. They can be expensive. They can be difficult to grow, so one should study the literature before trying to grow such gems as *L. canadense*, perhaps the most graceful, but not for light quick-draining soils. Returning to *Lilium auratum*, there are now some superb hybrids between this species and *L. speciosum*. The red of the latter species has been introduced into *L. auratum*, and without reducing the enormous size of the blooms. These new pink or red forms of *L. auratum* are not cheap, but like most lilies they can be raised from seed, and this makes them much less costly.

Indeed if one wants to grow lilies in generous numbers, and if one has patience, it is far better to raise them from seed. Unfortunately the lily suffers from virus diseases. The lily growers are trying hard to breed varieties immune from or resistant to these viruses. In our own gardens we do much to protect lilies from virus diseases by keeping the greenfly under control, because they spread the virus from plant to plant. There are plenty of aphis-killing insecticides on the market, and if they are used once a week from May to September, they will keep the aphis under control.

But the lilies grown from seed start off free from virus disease. One seedsman's catalogue lists over sixty species and varieties of lilies, including such gems as Kingdon Ward's discovery, *Lilium mackliniae*, named after his wife, the 'Oregon Hybrids', 'Belling-ham Hybrids', and many more.

Raising lilies from seed is not difficult. The species and varieties vary considerably in the time taken to produce a flowering sized bulb: some, like varieties of the white *L. longiflorum*, may flower within a year of sowing. Seeds are sown in any normal seed sowing compost, in pans or boxes, and are given plenty of room – an inch apart each way. I keep mine in a greenhouse until they have germinated, and then put them in a cold frame until the following spring; then I either pot up the small bulbs that have formed, or plant them out.

Some people claim that germination is better if the seeds are placed edgewise in the soil, but I have never been able to prove or disprove this. The lily is remarkable in the number of ways by which it can be increased. In many lilies small bulbils appear in the axils of the leaves, such as in *L. tigrinum*, *L. sargentiae*, and many of the modern hybrids. The tiny bulbils are left on the plants as long as possible in the late summer, but must be watched carefully and gathered before they fall off. Then they are 'sown' in a seed sowing compost, just covered with soil, and kept in a greenhouse or frame until the plants are large enough either to be potted up or planted out.

Some lilies produce small bulblets at the base of the stem just above the old bulbs. These bulblets can be removed in the autumn and grown on.

Yet another method of propagation is by removing some of the scales from the parent bulbs. These, if planted as recommended for the bulblets or bulbils, will eventually produce new bulbs, but it is a trickier method than the others.

People who live on inhospitable clay often grow lilies in tubs. A friend who has done so with great success, tells me that he removes the top inch or two of soil each year and replaces it with a layer of Clavering horse-manure compost – the mushroom compost which, as it contains no lump chalk, is proving excellent for mulching and for working into the ground at planting time.

Many people are under the impression that after a crop of mushrooms has been taken from the horse-manure compost, its food value is greatly reduced. This is not so, as experiments over a period of six years at Stockbridge Experimental Horticultural Station showed. The yields per acre of cauliflowers, carrots and leeks were in almost every trial higher where mushroom compost had been used than when fresh farmyard manure had been ploughed in. One great advantage of mushroom compost is that it is weed-free; also, as it has been thoroughly composted, it becomes available to the plants immediately, and having virtually no smell it is pleasant to handle. Although it is slightly alkaline, I have found no ill-effects with rhododendrons after repeated mulchings, but I would not recommend it at this stage for digging into ground where lime-hating plants are to be grown.

Restricting the root run

IF one has the time and patience one can play clever tricks with plants.

Only in favourable summers does my passion flower fruit, and then it produces only ornamental orange 'plums', quite inedible. It is not of course derived from the same species that provided the passion fruit juice with which we used to dilute our gin back in the thirties. Sometimes a passion flower fails to bloom if it is in too shaded a position, or if it is living on too lush a diet.

Like the fig, if you want it to fruit well, you restrict its root run and keep it on meagre rations. Anyone who has eaten the huge purple St John's figs in Malta will know that they grow in dry rocky spots, and receive scant attention from the Maltese.

So, too, with the passion flower. Plant it in shallow, rather poor soil – if necessary dig a hole about 18 in. deep and put in six inches of broken bricks, and then fill up with soil. If the plant is already established, try digging a trench two or three feet around it, and filling it to a depth of a couple of feet with bricks. This restriction of the roots may jerk it into flower.

Often one can quite unthinkingly do something silly – for example if a hydrangea has become too big, rather gaunt, and leggy, the temptation is to cut it right down to the ground. It will produce plenty of new growths all right, but in the following year there will be no flowers. A better way is to·cut out half the stems one year and the other half the next. Thus one will have, for two years, at least half a crop of flowers.

One can play the same trick on an apple tree that has got into the biennial bearing habit – that is, it carries a huge crop one year and takes the next year off. Remove the flowers from half the branches in an 'on' year, and then remove the flowers from the other half the next year. I have known this trick to work excellently.

There are tricks, too, with planting herbaceous paeonies, which must not be planted deeply, only so that there is not more than an inch of soil over the dormant growth buds. If one goes on adding mulches of one kind or another to the border, and the paeonies fail to flower, it is probable that these buds have now been buried too deeply, and one should scrape away some of the top soil.

The lovely flame flower, *Tropaeolum speciosum*, which scrambles with abandon over trees and shrubs, particularly in Scotland, is another plant that needs a little understanding. Thousands of roots have been sold and failed to grow. The trick is to plant the peculiar piece of root so that both ends are in the soil but the middle is above ground. Just weight it down with a large stone on its middle. The odds are it will grow lustily.

Then many people fail to persuade seeds of alpine plants to germinate. They are too kind to them; they sow them in a greenhouse, and keep them too warm. Sow the seeds now in pots or boxes, and put them outside to get all the frost and snow of the winter, just as they would on their native mountainside. They will probably grow thickly in the spring. We have a few candelabra primulas in one shady spot, and after the bad winter of 1962–3 the ground beneath them was covered with thousands of self-sown seedlings. It had never happened before, and has never happened since. This was one small dividend from a winter that I hope never to see repeated as long as I am trying to keep a garden in trim.

Taking a chance

HARDINESS is a relative term. Some plants are vulnerable to frost in their early years. Others are more liable to be killed or damaged by searing cold winds than by low temperatures. But for a great many more, the critical factor is excessive wet around the roots.

Many alpines come into this category; they would normally pass the winter under a friendly blanket of snow, but in this country even in a mild winter waterlogging of the roots is fatal. It may not be very attractive to have cloches or pieces of glass propped up all over the rock garden, but such protection would save the life of many a rock plant, particularly those with grey hairy foliage which seem particularly vulnerable.

If one likes to gamble with borderline plants, at least one can take precautions. At this time of year we tie the leaves of our red hot pokers into a kind of cone. This prevents too much water from lying in the crown of the plant. Then a wet season is the slugs' paradise. Preventive action now could pay dividends – weathered sharp gritty coke ashes spread liberally around cut-down plants of delphiniums and others that slugs dote upon. This covering of ashes needs to be stirred now and then, and any fallen leaves removed. Also a dose of slug pellets, preferably those containing 4 or 5 per cent metaldehyde, is a useful insurance against trouble later on.

There is always considerable divergence of opinion whether or not to leave outdoor chrysanthemums to overwinter in the ground. Some people do so and are successful. In my own garden, whenever I have tried it I have lost the lot, and mine is a very well drained garden. I lift my plants at this time of the year, wash all the soil off the roots and bed them in fresh soil in deep boxes which we keep throughout the winter under the bench of a glass-to-the-ground greenhouse. A cold frame, rugged up with sacking or similar protection on bitter nights, will do, but since we have the greenhouse space, we overwinter our chrysanthemums there.

It is important, however, not to forget them and to see that they are kept nicely moist throughout the winter.

Jobs for November

IF the weather is open, this is the month to make a great effort and clean the garden up. Sweep up fallen leaves and stack them, or add them to the compost heap. Be meticulous about clearing them from lawns, as, if left, they can quickly spoil the turf. Pay particular attention to gutters and open drains, clearing the leaves before they choke the outlets.

If the sight of old stems on herbaceous borders offends, cut them down now. If not, leave them until the spring. They will help to protect the plants from frosts. Make new plantings if required.

Plant, or divide and replant herbaceous plants if necessary. All the tap-rooted plants such as lupins and anchusas are best moved in the autumn: the fibrous-rooted plants, like phloxes or michaelmas daisies, may be left until the spring.

Climbers growing in borders with other plants may need a good feed – 6 to 8 oz. of bone meal or John Innes base fertiliser worked into the top few inches of soil. A good heavy mulch of dung around the plants, but not, of course, touching the stems, would help to stimulate strong new growths next year, if these have not been produced in sufficient quantity.

Press on with bulb planting in bowls and in the open.

If spring bedding plants have not been planted out by this time, leave them in their present quarters until the spring. The ground is colder now and they would probably suffer in severe spells if moved.

Check and renew ties on trees and climbers. Replace any stakes or posts that may be partially rotted – they rot most quickly just at, or slightly below, ground level. Renew or rewrite any labels before they become illegible and you have forgotten the name of the plant. If climbing or rambling roses have not been pruned, and the new growths tied in, do not delay any longer. Long shoots on hybrid teas and floribundas may be shortened by half their length to prevent high winds from rocking them about. Final pruning may be done next month, or in cold districts, next spring.

Lift dahlias as soon as the foliage is blackened by frost. If not already done, lift geraniums, begonias and fuchsias, and place them in a frost-proof place.

Trim back any plants in the rock garden that are encroaching upon their neighbours, or such as helianthemums, or dwarf hypericums, that are becoming leggy. Some rock plants, such as saxifrages and sedums that grow in mats or mounds, may benefit from some fine soil worked in among the growths. Remove weeds, and if stone chippings are used on the surface, renew these if necessary.

Gather up leaves and put them on the compost heap; those from fruit trees or roses that may be carrying disease should be burned.

Give the lawn the last cut and send the mower off for servicing if necessary.

Rake the lawn vigorously with a wire rake. If moss is present apply a mercuric moss-killer. If worms are active, water the lawn with a worm eradicant.

Weeds among shrubs and under hedges may be destroyed by watering with paraquat, or if much couch grass is present, give a treatment with dalapon.

If you have fish in a pool, consider installing a small immersion heater in the pool to keep a small area free of ice. They are quite cheap and simple to install.

Sow peas and broad beans under cloches.

December

I always look upon December as a kind of interim month in the steady rhythm of the gardener's round. With luck we have done the essential tasks of clearing up, planting and turning over the ground. If not, there is still time. But the euphoria of Christmas is already upon us. The seed catalogues, like the travel brochures, arrive earlier every year. There is dropping of hints about the presents that would be acceptable – sophisticated tools, the rather expensive plants that perhaps the family might rise to, but which they would probably have frowned upon if they had been bought in the ordinary way.

Then the bulbs in bowls are probably about ready to bring indoors and, especially where there are children in the family, there is the excitement of decorating the home for Christmas.

We may take a breather now, if all has gone well and look forward to another gardener's round with pleasurable anticipation knowing there will be failures and frustrations but also an abundance of pleasures.

Gifts for gardeners

PERHAPS more in the garden than in the home or with personal effects, a recipient is vastly delighted with a gift that he would have thought too extravagant to buy for himself. Over the years I have acquired a collection of expensive cigarette lighters, but the half-crown job, bought in Paris and made in Czecho-Slovakia, is the one that gives least trouble. Yet in the garden, presents that have given me the greatest pleasure are the tools that I would never have bought for myself, the stainless steel fork and spade, hand trowel and hand fork, hoe, lawn edger, rust-resisting pruners, and the like. These are available in various ranges in all good garden shops and some, such as Wilkinson shears, pruners, trowels and the like, are offered in attractive packs.

I would particularly recommend the narrow bulb-planting trowels: these, in stainless steel if you wish, are marked along the blade in inches, greatly facilitating the planting of bulbs at the correct depth. Further, these narrow trowels are much less fatiguing on the muscles and tendons of the wrist. Most often, when planting bulbs or small seedlings, it is not necessary to take out a hole as large as the normal-sized trowel would make. The weight of soil lifted by a bulb trowel is about a quarter of that moved by a large trowel. My wife, years ago, developed tenosinovitis in her wrist after planting hundreds of bulbs with a normal trowel. If she had used a narrow one, perhaps she would have avoided it. A bulb-planter and a narrow two-pronged hand fork come in an attractive pack at 57s 6d.

Once you have used stainless steel tools you will never wish to use any other. They are so easy to use, and easy to clean. They are expensive, but will last a lifetime. We are still using a stainless steel spade given to my father in 1930 by the Corporation of Sheffield, and it is almost as good as new.

Much garden work consists of moving rubbish, weeds, leaves, grass mowings and the like from one place to another. Of course one can often greatly reduce the barrowing time by creating the dump, suitably screened with shrubs, at one side in the middle of the garden instead of at the traditional far end. If it is possible to site the tool shed there too, much unnecessary journeying is saved when you need some tool, bamboo cane, or other essential.

With gardeners costing now about 3*d* a minute, minutes count. The single-wheeled metal or plastic barrow is still useful for narrow paths or for wheeling manure along a broad plank over soft soil. But the two-wheeled 'Joyride' truck, from 89*s* 6*d*, with a pram handle and a detachable body, is really a pleasure to use. I wrote about it years ago, and received a charming letter from a lady in roughly the following terms: 'I am delighted to have been put in touch with the two-wheeled truck. You see, I walk with a stick and I cannot manage a two-handled barrow. Now I am spared the ignominy of asking my gardener to empty my wheelbarrow.'

In many families Christmas provides the excuse for several members to club together to buy father or mother a fairly expensive item that he or she might hesitate to buy in the ordinary way. A very welcome addition to the gardener's equipment would be a battery mower – 12-, 14- or 18-in. size.

Just now, too, with the seed sowing season upon us in about eight weeks an electrically heated frame would be a greatly valued gift. One can buy now a wooden frame with two lights, ready equipped with air- and soil-warming wires, with thermostat control and which operates from a 13-amp socket in the house. It can be placed just outside the house, on the terrace, or outside the french windows, to be used for spring propagations, and then in mid-May, when it has done its work, it can be unplugged and stored in the garage until it is needed again.

Now I turn to the most illogical of all presents for a gardener – nesting boxes, feeding tables, and cylindrical wire feeders for filling with nuts for the birds. The 'Wendy' range of these items, available from E. J. Woodman & Sons Ltd, High Street, Pinner, Middlesex, is attractive, especially to children, and not expensive.

The nesting box costs 18s 6d or 27s 6d for the larger model; the bird table 17s 6d and the wire bird feeder 5s: all prices include postage.

At this season of good will, I hesitate to start an argument as to whether putting out food and water for birds distracts them from attacking buds on our fruit trees, or whether it merely attracts more birds to the garden. Birds give us enormous pleasure – they try our patience, but we do all we can to care for them in winter.

Gardening gloves are always welcome. There are many types available now – real tough ones for pruning, and ladies' gloves in man-made fibre, reasonably waterproof yet thin enough to allow small weeds, thin seedlings, and so on to be pulled up. Prices range from 10s 6d to just over £1. A really valuable gift that would give the recipient service over many years is a Dymo Label-maker. It makes embossed lettering on adhesive plastic tape which is weatherproof and long-lasting. The machine costs 79s 6d, or with ten spools of coloured tape, £6 15s.

As one grows older, bending and crouching become most arduous. Kneeling is uncomfortable unless one uses the rubber knee protectors, also from Woodmans of Pinner, or from garden shops costing 25s post paid. They are now fitted with the Velcro instant fastener; you just press the ends of each strap together, and they grip immediately. To take them off you give a sharp tug to one end of a strap.

The Easi-kneeler stool at £2 19s 6d with strong tubular steel legs, is either a stool, or when turned upside down is excellent for kneeling upon – the upturned legs enable the infirm to heave themselves up or down easily.

Greenhouse owners, especially if the greenhouse is equipped with electricity, would greatly appreciate an electrically heated propagating case. It makes the rooting of cuttings and seed germination much easier. The Big Top propagator at £31 18s 6d is probably the best value for money, and I am glad to say is finding a valuable export demand.

There is no end to the possibilities of giving pleasure to plant lovers. The self-watering plastic Riviera troughs or window boxes are most acceptable. They come in ivory, black or red. They can be used in the living room on a window, or a windowsill, and there are wrought iron stands in which the trough can be placed.

The self-watering principle really works: one filling of the reservoir in the base will keep plants going for two to three weeks. Prices range from £2 2s to £4 16s according to size, and wrought iron bases from 22s 6d to £4 6s according to trough size.

Turning from garden sundries to plants, I would suggest that a few of the modern American hybrid lilies would be most welcome. They are not cheap, but they should increase with the years and again are gifts that because they are rather pricey would be that much more acceptable. A flowering cherry, or a 'family' fruit tree, with four varieties of apple or pear grafted upon it, is a gift that would grow more valuable with the years.

Theoretically if a friend or relation is fond of gardening it should be easy to choose a Christmas present that will please. Sometimes, however, it is difficult to know exactly what to buy, as gardening tastes are so individual that what delights one person is anathema to another. Provided one has a fair idea of what the recipient likes, and what is already established in his garden, it should be possible to send a gift of plants or bulbs. House plants can be a mixed blessing unless one knows how well the recipient will look after them – or if indeed he or she wants to be bothered with them.

For a Christmas gift I would suggest an order is placed now for one or two of the cyclamen with white and green marbled leaves. They come in a good range of colours, and are easier to manage in the hot, dry atmosphere of the modern house than the old green-leaved varieties. Or one could order a pot of the brilliant scarlet *Poinsettia* 'Paul Mikkelsen'. In a sunny window it will keep attractive for months. This variety is a real break-through with poinsettias, which have, up to now, been almost impossible to manage in a living room.

If the choice of a gardening gift is too difficult, then one can always buy a garden gift token for a minimum of 10s 6d. The card, quite attractive, costs 6d, and to this is affixed the 10s stamp. Other stamps can be affixed to make the token worth any amount you may wish to give. These tokens may be purchased or exchanged at any one of many garden shops, garden centres, or nurseries, for any horticultural item they stock.

House plants

HORTICULTURE, it must be admitted, tends to be conservative, so it is heartening to report a successful development in this field. In the past few years the firm of Thomas Rochford and Sons in Hertfordshire has completely revolutionised its business and is now almost certainly the largest producer in the world of pot plants for the home. The firm produces four million house plants a year, yet so great is the demand that it has to turn down many orders. The market for house plants in Britain is really in its infancy, at least compared with that in Holland and Scandinavian countries. Cut flowers, of course, will always be in demand, but more and more people are realising that a pot plant will go on giving pleasure for years.

The Rochford story is fascinating. Years ago the nurseries produced grapes, tomatoes and cucumbers, but now 26 acres of glass and 300 employees produce nothing but house plants. Another four acres of greenhouses are in the course of erection. One is tempted to say that this is a plant factory – a production line for plants. So it is in some ways. Certainly, every modern device that can cut down manual work is used. All the plants are grown in plastic pots. Automatic watering is gradually being extended throughout the nursery. Indeed Rochfords have evolved a new watering system which is now being exported to many countries abroad. They even export their plants as well to places as far away as Bermuda, Beirut, Mauritius and Kuwait.

But producing plants is not quite the same as producing motor cars or washing machines. Automation is a wonderful aid but the horticultural know-how is essential. The techniques of propagation are also all-important. It is interesting to see, for example, thousands of leaf cuttings of *Begonia rex* in one of the propagating houses. The leaves are cut into pieces about the size of a postage stamp and laid on special compost on warm benches. After some weeks a tiny plant begins to grow from the end of a cut vein. Most varieties will produce a plant from this piece of leaf laid flat on the compost. Others like *Begonia masoniana* need to be inserted vertically in the compost.

Then Rochfords have evolved a technique of labelling their plants when they go to the shops. Different coloured labels are used to indicate how easy or how difficult the particular plant may be to keep growing happily in the home. The easy varieties – *Philodendron scandens*, *Ficus decora*, the rubber plant, sansevieria, which is almost impossible to kill, tradescantias and many more – carry a pink label. The more exacting plants that need a constant temperature of between 50° F and 60° F, such as *Peperomia caperata*, various marantas, scindapsuses, and so on, carry a blue label, and the delicate plants which usually have a short life under normal home conditions have a yellow label – saintpaulias, anthuriums, crotons, and the like. But even these can be grown for years if one is prepared to cosset them with higher temperatures and close attention to their need for watering and humidity.

At this time of year millions of pot plants will be sold. Many will survive but many more will die a lingering death. Azaleas are grown in almost pure peat. If this dries out it is virtually impossible to wet it again by watering from above. The only way is to stand the pot in a bucket of water for an hour or so. The cyclamen is another tricky plant. Kept in a cool room, where the temperature is normally not more than 60° F, it will grow and flower happily. In higher temperatures its leaves will soon turn yellow because in the home the atmosphere is not moist enough.

At this time of year many firms offer Christmas gift packs of hyacinth bulbs already well started into growth which one can order to be sent through the post to a friend. And any florist can arrange for a bowl of house plants to be sent. These bowls of pot plants will grow well for nine months; after that one or two plants may outgrow the bowl and it will need replanting. But such a bowl, giving nine months of pleasure, is a wonderful gift.

In the winter, foliage plants in the home need very little water but plenty of light. They may be moved near the windows. But the leaves of foliage plants may soon become covered with a thick layer of dust. This should be wiped off with a damp cloth. And if you want the foliage to shine it should be wiped, after cleaning, with Bio Leafshine. This puts a wonderful gloss on the leaves without interfering with their natural function. The Rochford foliage plants are all sprayed, before leaving the nursery, with a solution of thin liquid paraffin, like the medicinal paraffin. Two tablespoonfuls in two gallons of tepid water, thoroughly stirred, give the leaves a wonderful gloss.

If I were to choose a house plant to give as a present I would plump for one of the varieties of *Begonia rex* or for *B. masoniana*. In spite of the fact that they are classified as delicate and wear a yellow label I have found them extremely easy to keep happy in our old farmhouse where the temperature may fluctuate from less than 60° F to even more than 70° F.

For a gorgeous show over Christmas and well into January or February the scarlet 'Mikkelsen' poinsettia is a winner. Strangely, the demand for pink or white poinsettias is negligible. Apparently the public has the mistaken idea that the pink variety is just a scarlet one that is in the process of fading. But I can imagine many rooms where the pink or white forms would blend more effectively than the scarlet form.

Ferns stage a comeback

RECENT writings about ferns have brought interesting correspondence with readers, confirming my impression that they are on the verge of a comeback. The demand has stimulated production, and it appears that ferns will be seen more frequently in our homes and gardens. Exhibits of tender ferns at recent Royal Horticultural Society shows have aroused great interest. With the steady increase in the number of greenhouses being built in amateurs' gardens, and the growing popularity of the sun porch, ferns will undoubtedly find their place.

Either in a greenhouse or in the home, they need plenty of moisture and shade from strong sun. This is often easier to supply in a greenhouse than in a home, especially if the home is centrally heated. But as with many house plants, the problem of moisture in the atmosphere can be overcome by standing the pots on plastic trays, which are filled with pebbles and always kept partially full of water. Even better from an aesthetic viewpoint is to plunge the pot in peat in some attractive container -- a copper jam pan or coal bucket, a small wooden chest with a metal lining, or something similar. If the peat and the soil in the pots are kept watered the atmosphere around the ferns is sufficiently moist to prevent undue transpiration from their fronds. These greenhouse ferns are very satisfying to grow, because even the small plants in $2\frac{1}{2}$ in. pots grow quickly and soon need to be transferred into $4\frac{1}{2}$ in. pots. Varieties of pteris, nephrolepis, adiantum and asplenium, are all ferns well worth trying for the greenhouse or the home.

In the greenhouse one has to remember that they do not like B.H.C. sprays, or fumigant 'smokes', or B.H.C. fumigation such as is provided by the eletrically operated vaporisers.

In twelve years since we installed electric vaporisers we have never seen white fly in our houses, this in spite of the fact that we have grown many plants the white fly thrive on, including the lemon-scented verbena, which is one of their favourites.

Turning to the hardy ferns, there is the point that they need shade, or in many cases, partial shade – that is, shade during most of the day. Most gardens are able to provide such conditions, or it can be created by planting suitable trees and shrubs. Indeed the ferns will often furnish a shaded spot where it is difficult to establish anything else, and if the site should be unduly dry, it is a simple matter, in these days of semi-rigid plastic pipe and a multitude of watering devices, to supply the necessary moisture without much effort.

Hardy ferns, too, are long-suffering plants, in that they grow with equanimity in town or country. Naturally they luxuriate in the damp shade of a woodland garden, but they will still give great pleasure in a little courtyard of a town house.

Some, like hart's tongue fern, *Scolopendrium vulgare*, will grow almost anywhere. Some plants that we prised out of stone walls in Devonshire have grown happily in full sun on the edge of our rock garden for ten years and, presumably, will go on growing indefinitely. They are watered, of course, along with the rest of the rock garden, in summer when we run into dry periods. There is a variety with wavy edges – *S.v. crispum* 'Nobile'. Another fern that will grow well in a sunny situation, or in semi-shade, is *Pellaea atropurpurea*, which has leathery fronds in shades of green. It is evergreen, and is a good species to grow where the soil is inclined to be limey. Indeed, it is wise to add lime to the soil to keep it happy.

The Christmas fern, *Polystichum acrostichoides*, evergreen, hence its common name, is another lovely species. So, too, is *Athyrium filix-foemina*, the lady fern. But perhaps the most graceful of them all is the hardy maidenhair fern *Adiantum pedatum*. This is the hardy counterpart of the maidenhair fern we grow in greenhouses, and if it is well sited in damp semi-shade, soon makes a large and handsome plant. There is a lovely variety *japonicum*. In the spring when the first fronds unfold they are rose coloured and gradually change to bronze, and then to green.

I have often enthused about the 'waste paper basket' or 'ostrich feather' fern. It grows upright like a large shuttlecock, to a height of two or three feet depending on the soil conditions. It grows best in moist shade, but I know gardens where it has almost naturalised itself, and often in full sun. Certainly in full sun the plants are not so lush as in cool damp shade. Its official name now is *Matteuccia struthiopteris.* The male fern, *Dryopteris filix-mas,* is another easy-going species in damp shade.

It is perhaps unfortunate that the ferns have such daunting Latin names. They all have common names as well, but few people know them. Their common names are usually quite charming – the hard shield fern, the cliff brake, the cinnamon fern, the giant wood fern, and so on. But it would be a pity if the Latin names put any gardener off growing these charming and equable plants. They never suffer from pests or diseases – at least in my experience – and they ask no more than the removal of the dead fronds at some time before growth starts in the spring.

Where are the Christmas roses?

MANY of us, full of good intentions, forget to plant deliberately for the winter months. I do not propose to involve myself in defining when winter begins and ends. E. A. Bowles in his delightful book *My Garden in Autumn and Winter* had difficulty enough in reconciling the seasons of the astronomers and the ordinary citizen's conception of them. Rather I would think about the plants that one can have in flower at Christmas or shortly after in gardens in all but the least favoured localities.

Of course one thinks of the Christmas rose, *Helleborus niger,* but something strange has happened to this plant. Time was when the great gardens had a lavish border of Christmas roses that really flowered for Christmas, and the blooms were used in their hundreds for decorating the house. Now a plant that flowers thus early is a variety E. A. Bowles describes as *Helleborus niger praecox*, a name I fail to find in any modern catalogue, and I quote his comments: 'The first Hellebore flower of autumn is always borne by an early-flowering form of the Christmas rose, *Helleborus niger praecox*, which generally begins flowering in the end of September. Its large white flowers are so lovely that in spite of its unseasonableness, I should like to have more than the one clump that has not increased very much, though it has lived in a cosy corner of the rock garden for many years.'

He also described a form that he received from 'the wooded hillside above Menaggio or Cadenabbia, I forget which', and which produced large and perfect flowers in November. Funds and travel allowances permitting, I must take a trip one autumn to the Italian lakes.

Frances Perry, who knew Mr Bowles well, and who still keeps an eye on his old garden at Myddelton House, tells me that all these early-flowering hellebores have disappeared, yet the forms of *H. altifolius*, *H. lividus* and *H. orientalis* are still flourishing. There is even still the form of *H. orientalis* with almost black flowers which was Bowles' pride and joy. She also tells me that some years ago she saw a nursery in Sweden in November where there were plantations of *Helleborus niger* sheeted with white flowers. Let us hope that somebody with time to spare will reintroduce a Christmas-flowering Christmas rose.

Another strange thing about the Christmas rose. Usually, when the plants are divided, the first flowering of the division produces pink flowers. Thereafter the flowers are white once more.

Another puzzle to me is *Iris unguicularis* or, before the botanists renamed it, *Iris stylosa*. We have some large clumps in front of the house, but hardly ever a flower. All the plantsmen that come to see us give us advice. Maybe slugs are eating the buds. Perhaps the plants need lime. Perhaps the foliage should be cut down in summer. Maybe they dry out under the house wall. We have mulched, fed bone meal, watered – all to no avail.

When we get time we will lift and divide the plants and put a few in a dozen different parts of the garden. Then maybe we shall have flowers for our Christmas dinner table. Incidentally, it is fun to pick them in bud and have them on the breakfast table near an electric toaster. One can then watch the flowers flick open, a petal at a time – guaranteed to amuse.

At this time we cut fairly lavishly from a large bush of *Viburnum fragrans*. It is a fast grower – in a north-facing border behind a wall it is now a good ten feet high after only about eight years. It is a good shrub for a mixed border, as it is upright in habit yet generous with its side branches, and I never mind how much my wife cuts off it, as this indiscriminate pruning just seems to encourage it to make more side growths. The form we have is a good pink, and came as a young plant from that great gardener the late A. T. Johnson, who for so many years wrote anonymously for *The Times*. The ordinary forms are rather more white than pink, and there is a white, sweetly scented form 'Candidissima' which is well worth growing. So too is *V. bodnantense* 'Charles Lamont' another Christmas flower, deep pink and very generous with its blossoms.

In odd corners of the garden are plants of *Iris foetidissima*, and these chance seedings we leave because we use the opened seed pods filled with their orange-scarlet seeds in our winter flower arrangements. Indeed, I always try to leave any self-sown seedling, if it is not in too impossible a place, because I take the view that if a plant really wants to grow there, it will grow well without much help from me.

Going back for a moment to that mine of information, E. A. Bowles' three volumes about his garden, I notice that he has wise advice about the winter jasmine, the yellow flowered *Jasminum nudiflorum*. We have it growing in a tangle on a wall along with *Cotoneaster horizontalis*. In some years when we have remembered to prune the jasmine hard after flowering, and when the birds have kindly refrained from stripping the berries from the cotoneaster, the combination of red and gold has been delightful. But Bowles suggests that the jasmine should be trained around three stakes and cut back each spring. He says that one gets better shoots for cutting in this way than one would get from a wall-trained plant. This is one more trick we will try.

Beware the bodgers

BEWARE the characters who call at houses offering to prune fruit trees. I heard of a case recently where a woman allowed one of these men to prune her three apple trees. The result was a disaster. He sawed all the branches back to leave snags about a foot or two long and charged her £20. When she asked if he was going to remove the cut-off branches he offered to make a bonfire of them for another £3. And he did not treat the cut surfaces with a bitumen preparation to stop infection: all tree wounds more than an inch across should be painted with one of these preparations.

The tragedy for this owner is that she will get no fruit next year or the year after and the trees will probably make a thicket of growths which will have to be very carefully dealt with eventually.

Far more damage is done to fruit trees by unnecessary or too drastic pruning than by neglect. Remember that pruning encourages new and often unwanted growth. If one has a lop-sided tree the temptation is to cut back the strong branches. This, of course, only encourages more growth and one should cut back the weak branches to persuade them to grow and balance the tree. If a fruit tree has arrived at a fruit-bearing stage, unless you want very high quality fruit leave it alone. Remove only branches that are rubbing against each other or cluttering up the centre of the tree, and any dead or diseased wood.

It is becoming increasingly difficult to find people to do odd jobs in the home or garden who know what they are doing. A friend recently acquired a house whose oak front door had been painted bright red by the previous incumbent. He asked a local odd job man if he would 'pickle off' the paint. He agreed to do so but wanted £20 for the job. When my friend demurred, he said, 'But it will take a whole day!'

There seems to be a good living to be made by any conscientious odd job men who know what they are doing, but although there are many instructional courses open to them, few seem to avail themselves of them. This is a problem that as far as I can see is going to become more acute as the old, retired gardeners who know their job gradually disappear.

Not difficult – only different

IT is unfortunate that orchids are often thought to be fabulously expensive plants and difficult to grow. This is not true. Of course there are rare and expensive orchids, just as there are rare and expensive postage stamps. Of course some – indeed many – of them require fairly high temperatures, over 55° F night minimum, but there are hundreds of varieties of cymbidium, for example, that need only what we call 'frost protection' – that is, a night minimum of 45° F. Even these plants will support the occasional night when the temperature falls below this figure, so long as it does not fall below freezing.

The cultivation of orchids generally is not difficult, merely different from the ordinary run of plants we grow in greenhouses. In Nature some orchids grow in the ground – they are known as terrestrial orchids – and others grow on the branches of trees, and are known as epiphytes. In the greenhouse most orchids are grown in a mixture of osmunda fibre and sphagnum moss, which can be obtained from the better garden firms, or from the specialist orchid nurseries. The cymbidiums and cypripediums, which are probably the best for the amateur to start with, like a little well-decayed fibrous loam added to these ingredients.

As a race the British are notoriously 'hit and miss'. When we buy a new machine we only read the instructions if we cannot put it together, or make it work. When gardening we tend to rely first on our limited experience even in attempting to grow new plants, and only when they fail to grow do we seek advice or refer to a book. The majority of garden plants are so long-suffering that most of the time we achieve reasonable results in this way, but I would strongly urge anyone who is tempted to grow a few orchids to buy a book on the subject, and start off in the right way.

The illusion that orchids are only for the rich has been maintained over the years by the book publishers. Reichenbach's famous hand-coloured monograph of orchids is now a museum piece, an *objet d'art*. Then in the middle of last century B. S. Williams produced *The Orchid Grower's Manual*, which ran to several editions. It was, of course, cheap by comparison, but even now his seventh edition may fetch £8 or £9. Later Charles Curtis produced *Orchids for Everyone*, and just before the war revised it under the title *Orchids*, which sold even then for four guineas.

Then the *Encyclopaedia of Cultivated Orchids*, by Alex D. Hawkes (Faber), appeared, price 12 guineas. This is a massive, comprehensive and valuable work which describes all the orchids known to be in cultivation today. It is well illustrated in colour and monochrome, and will be eagerly sought by every serious orchid grower throughout the world, and there are many thousands today.

Of course this is not a book for a beginner. For him *Orchids for Everyone*, by O. Eigeldinger (John Gifford, 25s), is of enormous help. Mr Eigeldinger explains how easy it is to succeed with orchids, and I would think his book is guaranteed not only to persuade the reader to take the plunge into orchid growing but also, if his advice is followed, to ensure success.

It is often said that one has to devote a whole greenhouse to orchids, that one cannot grow other plants with them. This is not quite true, but to get the best out of the orchids one must, of course, create in the greenhouse the ideal conditions for them and then choose other plants that like the same conditions.

Ideally one should be able to provide three different temperatures in three different sections of the greenhouse to be able to grow a really representative range of orchids. This is not difficult these days, when it is possible to subdivide a greenhouse with plastic sheeting and to provide additional heating in different sections by means of electrical equipment thermostatically controlled. Even if the original installation throughout the whole house is warmed by a coke or oil-fired boiler, the extra boost required is easily provided by electrical tubular heaters, or even fan-assisted heaters. Fan-assisted heaters have the advantage that they can be used to provide a certain amount of air movement in the house if the atmospheric conditions tend to be rather stagnant. They are portable and easily installed, but will need maintenance.

Apart from the great multiplicity of orchid species and hybrids, with their tremendous variation in shape, size and colouring, they have the advantage of flowering mainly in the winter and early spring, thus providing interest in the garden when there is little else in flower. Orchid blooms also last for a long time.

Perhaps more than any other group of plants, orchids exert a fascination all their own. In many ways they are the most rewarding plants that one can grow.

When winter comes

IN anything about the British weather, as it concerns gardeners at least, I am a confirmed pessimist. One November, coming out of Paris on the Golden Arrow, for an hour all the trees, even the tall poplars, were covered with white frost. The effect was charming, but in the restaurant car the French were exclaiming that they had never seen such a thing in November, and they were gloomy in their forebodings for winter.

I should, of course, have accepted the warning, and taken evasive action, but the once-vivid memories of our troubles in the 1962–3 winter have been dimmed by succeeding mild winters. However, here are a few reminders of precautions we could take to avoid trouble in periods of snow and frost.

Newly planted evergreens should be protected against north and east winds; straw or bracken placed over them temporarily, and removed when mild weather returns, is the most obvious method, but a more permanent screen of branches of conifers or the like, stuck in the ground around the plants, is useful. So, too, is a screen of plastic fixed to canes: this will give excellent shelter. It is unwise, however, to cover plants completely with plastic unless the top can be opened in mild weather.

I often wonder how the huge bay trees behind the American Embassy at the corner of the Place de la Concorde are revealed refreshed and unharmed each spring, after passing the winter in a close-fitting overcoat of thick hessian. They can presumably breathe through the covering.

Naturally, one of the worst problems is clearing snow from drives, entrances and the like. Where the area involved justifies it, some form of mechanised snow clearance is a great boon. There are snow plough attachments for the Autogardener cultivator at £16 16s, and at £7 for the Allen Scythe. The Toro range of snow blowers comes in three sizes from 49 guineas.

Also for the larger estate, if one is contemplating buying one of the mini-tractors, it is worth remembering that besides its many other functions, it clears snow superbly.

It is unusual for us to have frosts hard enough to penetrate buildings and damage corms, tubers, and so on before Christmas, but it does happen. So it would be wise to see that all such vulnerable material is safe.

A part of a shed can be partitioned, and a thermostat-controlled blower heater installed to keep the temperature above freezing. One such heater installed in a loft can save much trouble in a really cold spell. I still do not understand why builders insist on placing water tanks in the loft. In our last home, we had the cold water tank mounted above the hot water tank in a cupboard on the landing, and it worked extremely well. My wife found it also an excellent airing cupboard.

And so to the end of the year's round. A happy Christmas and happier gardening in the New Year.

Jobs for December

To a large extent the gardener's work in December consists of doing what was not done in November. Finish cutting down herbaceous plants, clearing the borders of weeds and fallen leaves. Transplant and divide any plants in need of this treatment. Make new plantings and if any trees or shrubs are on order, prepare the ground for them. If any arrive and the ground is too wet or frosty for planting, or if you are having a dose of 'flu, have the bundles unpacked and keep the plants in a shed with their roots wrapped in damp sacking. Better still have them heeled in, out in some sheltered odd corner of the garden.

In the southern half of England and in mild districts elsewhere, roses may be pruned in December. Wait until late March in the north and in cold parts of the country.

Try to finish fruit-tree pruning by the end of the month. A spraying with a tar oil wash will greatly reduce pests next year. Deciduous ornamental trees and shrubs, prunus hedges, and the like would also benefit from a similar spraying. It would clear them of green algal growth. But choose a still day and one when frost is not expected. Burn all prunings. Collect and burn all brown decayed fruits from trees or from the ground underneath.

Place Scaraweb, the rayon spider's web material, on branches of fruit trees, forsythias, flowering cherries, wisterias, and any other plants from which the birds normally steal the buds. Watch for signs of mice, and set traps if necessary.

Look at the bulbs in bowls where they have been placed outside under a layer of peat, straw, or the like. If daffodils and tulips have made two inches of growth, and if the bud of the hyacinth is well clear of the neck of the bulb, they may be brought into the warmth and light gradually. If not, leave them where they are for another week or two.

Clean strawberry beds, removing dead leaves and any runners still left on the plants.

Protect globe artichoke plants; cut the stems down to almost 12 in., draw the soil up to them with a hoe, and pack straw around, but not over, them.

In the greenhouse and frames be scrupulous in removing decaying leaves and faded flowers. Dig up some roots of mint, and plant them in boxes of soil in the greenhouse.

Send off mowers and other machines for servicing. There are too many machines around now for the available mechanics to handle in a hurry in the spring.

Treat tools and machines with rust-proofing fluid – you can buy it in aerosol packs nowadays, so after washing the muck off tools and machines you can just spray it on. This is much easier than trying to oil all six blades of a mower by hand with an oily rag.

Take garden furniture under cover; if you have no shed space, wrap it in plastic sheeting.

Index